Social Skills For Kids: From Shy To Social Butterfly In 30 Days

Barley Nicola

Published by Barley Nicola, 2024.

SOCIAL SKILLS FOR KIDS: FROM SHY TO SOCIAL BUTTERFLY IN 30 DAYS

First edition. April 2, 2024.

Copyright © 2024 Barley Nicola.

ISBN: 979-8224647187

Written by Barley Nicola.

Table of Contents

Chapter 1: Introduction.. 1

Chapter 2: Building Self-Confidence.. 5

Chapter 3: Communication Skills 9

Chapter 4: Making Friends.. 13

Chapter 5: Conflict Resolution 17

Chapter 6: Empathy and Understanding Others 22

Chapter 7: Social Etiquette 25

Chapter 8: Dealing with Bullying 29

Chapter 9: Building Positive Relationships 33

Chapter 10: Overcoming Social Anxiety 37

Chapter 11: Teamwork and Collaboration.. 41

Chapter 12: Public Speaking and Presentation Skills 45

Chapter 13: Problem-Solving Skills 49

Chapter 14: Time Management and Organization 53

Chapter 15: Goal Setting and Achievement.. 57

Chapter 16; Developing Leadership Skills... 61

Chapter 17: Networking and Building Connections 64

Chapter 18: Social Media and Online Etiquette 68

Chapter 19: Diversity and Inclusion 71

Chapter 20: Conclusion... 75

Chapter 1: Introduction

- UNDERSTANDING THE importance of social skills for children

Social skills are a crucial aspect of a child's development, playing a significant role in their overall well-being and success in life. These skills encompass a wide range of abilities, including communication, empathy, cooperation, and conflict resolution. Children who possess strong social skills are better able to navigate social situations, build positive relationships, and establish a sense of belonging within their peer group. As such, it is essential for parents, educators, and caregivers to recognize the importance of fostering these skills in children from a young age.

One of the key benefits of developing social skills in children is the impact it has on their emotional and mental health. Strong social skills enable children to express their thoughts and feelings effectively, leading to better emotional regulation and stress management. Additionally, children with strong social skills are more likely to have a positive self-image and high self-esteem, as they are able to form meaningful connections with others and receive support and validation. Ultimately, these factors contribute to improved mental well-being and resilience in the face of adversity.

Furthermore, social skills play a crucial role in academic success. Children who have well-developed social skills are better able to collaborate with their peers, communicate effectively with teachers, and engage in group activities. This not only enhances their learning experience but also fosters a positive and supportive classroom environment. In addition, strong social skills are linked to better problem-solving abilities and critical thinking, as children learn to consider different perspectives and work together to find solutions. As a result, children who possess strong social skills are more likely to excel academically and achieve their full potential.

Moreover, social skills are essential for building and maintaining relationships throughout life. Children who learn how to communicate effectively, show empathy, and resolve conflicts peacefully are more likely to form healthy and lasting friendships. These relationships provide important sources of emotional support, companionship, and belonging, which are essential for mental well-being and overall happiness. Furthermore, strong social skills are crucial for success in the workplace, as they enable individuals to collaborate with colleagues, communicate effectively with clients, and navigate complex social dynamics. As such, teaching children social skills early on sets them up for success in all areas of their lives.

It is important to note that social skills are not innate abilities but can be learned and developed over time. Parents, educators, and caregivers play a key role in nurturing these skills through positive reinforcement, modeling appropriate behavior, and providing opportunities for children to practice and refine their social skills. Encouraging children to engage in cooperative play, participate in group activities, and take turns during conversations are just a few ways to support the development of social skills. Additionally, teaching children about empathy, active listening, and conflict resolution strategies can help them navigate social interactions more effectively. Strong social skills provide children with the tools they need to build positive relationships, communicate effectively, and navigate social situations with confidence. By fostering the development of these skills from a young age, parents, educators, and caregivers can help children thrive academically, emotionally, and socially. Ultimately, investing in the development of social skills in children is an investment in their future happiness and success.

- Exploring the challenges shy children face in social situations

Shyness is a common personality trait that can present challenges for children in social situations. While some children may naturally be more introverted or reserved, extreme shyness can impact a child's ability to interact with peers, participate in activities, and build friendships. It is important for parents, teachers, and other caregivers to recognize the challenges that shy children face and provide support to help them navigate social situations with confidence.

One of the main challenges that shy children face in social situations is difficulty initiating and maintaining conversations. Shy children may feel self-conscious or anxious when talking to others, leading them to avoid social interactions altogether. This can make it difficult for shy children to make friends and build relationships with their peers. In addition, shy children may struggle to assert themselves in group settings or stand up for themselves when faced with teasing or bullying. As a result, shy children may feel isolated or misunderstood, leading to feelings of loneliness and low self-esteem.

Another challenge that shy children face in social situations is difficulty expressing their thoughts and feelings. Shy children may struggle to communicate effectively, leading to misunderstandings or misinterpretations of their intentions. This can make it difficult for shy children to form connections with others and engage in meaningful conversations. Shy children may also find it challenging to express their needs or advocate for themselves in social situations, leading to feelings of frustration or helplessness. It is important for caregivers to provide shy children with opportunities to practice communication skills and express themselves in a safe and supportive environment.

Shy children may also struggle with feelings of anxiety or fear in social situations. Shyness can be triggered by new or unfamiliar social situations, causing shy children to feel overwhelmed or stressed. This can lead to physical symptoms such as sweating, trembling, or rapid heartbeat, making it even more difficult for shy children to engage with others. Shy children may also avoid social situations that trigger feelings of anxiety, leading to missed opportunities for social growth and development. It is important for caregivers to help shy children manage their anxiety and build coping strategies to navigate social situations effectively.

In addition to these challenges, shy children may also face stigma or negative perceptions from others. Shyness is often misunderstood as aloofness or unfriendliness, leading to misunderstandings and misconceptions about shy children's intentions. As a result, shy children may be excluded or overlooked in social settings, making it even more difficult for them to build relationships with their peers. Caregivers can support shy children by educating others about the challenges of shyness and advocating for their needs in social situations. By raising awareness and promoting empathy, caregivers can help create a more inclusive and supportive environment for shy children to thrive.

Despite the challenges that shy children face in social situations, it is important to remember that shyness is a normal and valid part of a child's personality. Shy children have unique strengths and qualities that can contribute to their social interactions, such as empathy, creativity, and deep listening skills. By recognizing and celebrating these strengths, caregivers can help shy children build confidence and self-esteem in social situations. It is essential for caregivers to provide shy children with support, encouragement, and opportunities to practice social skills in a safe and nurturing environment. With patience and understanding, shy children can learn to navigate social situations with courage and resilience, building meaningful relationships and connections with others.

Chapter 2: Building Self-Confidence

- TECHNIQUES TO IMPROVE self-esteem and confidence in children

Self-esteem and confidence are critical aspects of a child's emotional and psychological development. Children who possess healthy self-esteem are more likely to have a positive self-image, experience greater academic success, and exhibit higher levels of resilience in the face of challenges. Similarly, confidence is essential for children to navigate social interactions, pursue their goals, and handle peer pressure effectively. As parents, educators, and caregivers, it is crucial to nurture and support children in building their self-esteem and confidence from a young age. Fortunately, there are several techniques and strategies that can help enhance these essential qualities in children.

One of the most effective ways to enhance a child's self-esteem and confidence is through the use of positive reinforcement. Praise and encouragement play a vital role in boosting a child's self-worth and belief in their abilities. When a child receives recognition for their efforts and achievements, they feel valued and competent, leading to a positive self-perception. It is essential to provide specific and genuine praise to the child, highlighting the skills and qualities that they have demonstrated. Avoiding generalized or excessive praise can prevent a child from becoming overly reliant on external validation and instead foster a sense of internal confidence and self-worth.

Another technique to improve self-esteem and confidence in children is by helping them set realistic and achievable goals. Goal-setting allows children to develop a sense of purpose, direction, and accomplishment. By breaking down larger goals into smaller, manageable steps, children can experience success and build confidence gradually. Encouraging children to identify their strengths, interests, and values can help them set goals that are aligned with their personal aspirations. It is essential to support children in setting goals that are challenging yet attainable, as this balance can promote growth and self-efficacy.

In addition to setting goals, fostering a growth mindset in children is a powerful tool for enhancing self-esteem and confidence. A growth mindset is the belief that intelligence, abilities, and talents can be developed through effort, perseverance, and learning from mistakes. By promoting a growth mindset, children are more likely to embrace challenges, persist in the face of setbacks, and view failure as an opportunity for growth. Encouraging children to adopt a positive attitude towards learning and problem-solving can help them build resilience, self-confidence, and a sense of agency over their own development.

Furthermore, cultivating a supportive and nurturing environment is essential for promoting positive self-esteem and confidence in children. Children thrive in environments where they feel safe, valued, and accepted for who they are. As parents and educators, it is crucial to provide consistent love, care, and attention to children, fostering a sense of belonging and security. By creating a supportive environment that encourages open communication, emotional expression, and empathy, children can develop strong social and emotional skills that contribute to their self-esteem and confidence.

Moreover, developing social skills and fostering positive relationships is another key strategy for enhancing self-esteem and confidence in children. Strong social bonds and connections contribute to a child's sense of identity, belonging, and self-worth. Encouraging children to engage in activities that promote cooperation, teamwork, and communication can help them build social confidence and resilience. Providing opportunities for children to practice conflict resolution, empathy, and assertiveness can enhance their interpersonal skills and self-esteem. By fostering positive relationships with peers, family members, and mentors, children can feel supported, valued, and accepted, boosting their self-esteem and confidence. By implementing techniques such as positive reinforcement, goal-setting, fostering a growth mindset, creating a supportive environment, and developing social skills, parents, educators, and caregivers can nurture and enhance these critical qualities in children. Building self-esteem and confidence in children requires patience, consistency, and empathy, as well as a deep understanding of their individual needs, strengths, and interests. By investing in the emotional and psychological development of children, we can empower them to navigate life's challenges with resilience, positivity, and confidence.

- Encouraging positive self-talk and self-acceptance

Encouraging positive self-talk and self-acceptance is crucial for overall mental health and well-being. Self-talk refers to the inner dialogue we have with ourselves, which can either be positive or negative. Positive self-talk involves encouraging and uplifting thoughts, while negative self-talk consists of self-criticism and doubt. Self-acceptance, on the other hand, involves recognizing and embracing all aspects of ourselves, including our strengths and weaknesses.

One of the first steps in promoting positive self-talk and self-acceptance is becoming aware of the thoughts and beliefs we hold about ourselves. Oftentimes, we may not even realize the negative messages we are sending ourselves on a daily basis. By taking the time to tune into our inner dialogue, we can start to identify patterns of negative self-talk and work towards changing them.

One effective strategy for promoting positive self-talk is to challenge and reframe negative thoughts. For example, if you catch yourself thinking, "I'm not good enough," try reframing that thought to, "I am capable and deserving of success." By consciously changing the way we talk to ourselves, we can start to shift our mindset towards a more positive and empowering outlook.

Another important aspect of encouraging positive self-talk and self-acceptance is practicing self-compassion. Self-compassion involves treating ourselves with kindness and understanding, especially in moments of struggle or self-doubt. Instead of berating ourselves for our mistakes or imperfections, we can offer ourselves words of encouragement and reassurance.

Additionally, surrounding ourselves with supportive and uplifting individuals can also help foster a more positive self-image. Having friends and loved ones who see and appreciate our worth can boost our self-esteem and reinforce a sense of self-acceptance. Seeking out a therapist or counselor can also be beneficial in working through deeper-seated issues that may be contributing to negative self-talk.

Ultimately, promoting positive self-talk and self-acceptance is an ongoing process that requires practice and patience. By cultivating a mindset of self-love and acceptance, we can create a more positive and fulfilling relationship with ourselves. Remember, you are deserving of love, respect, and compassion – both from others and from yourself.

Chapter 3: Communication Skills

- DEVELOPING EFFECTIVE ways to communicate with others

Effective communication is crucial in all aspects of life, whether it be in the workplace, in personal relationships, or even in casual interactions with strangers. Developing effective ways to communicate with others is essential for building strong connections, resolving conflicts, and achieving success in various endeavors. In this essay, we will explore the importance of communication, discuss the key components of effective communication, and provide practical tips on how to improve your communication skills.

Communication is the foundation of human interaction, allowing individuals to exchange thoughts, ideas, emotions, and information. Without effective communication, misunderstandings can arise, leading to confusion, conflict, and resentment. On the other hand, clear and concise communication can foster trust, empathy, and cooperation, enabling individuals to work together towards common goals. In the workplace, effective communication is essential for building strong teams, resolving conflicts, and achieving organizational objectives. In personal relationships, communication is key to building intimacy, resolving conflicts, and creating strong connections with others.

There are several key components of effective communication that are essential to consider when striving to improve one's communication skills. First and foremost, active listening is a crucial aspect of effective communication. This involves not only hearing what the other person is saying but also paying attention to their tone of voice, body language, and emotions. By actively listening to others, you can better understand their perspectives, feelings, and needs, enabling you to respond in a thoughtful and empathetic manner.

Another important component of effective communication is clarity and conciseness. It is essential to communicate your thoughts and ideas in a clear and straightforward manner, avoiding jargon, ambiguity, and unnecessary details. This helps to ensure that your message is easily understood by others, minimizing the risk of misunderstandings and misinterpretations. Additionally, using nonverbal cues such as eye contact, facial expressions, and gestures can enhance the clarity and impact of your communication, conveying sincerity, warmth, and empathy.

Furthermore, being mindful of your tone of voice and body language is key to effective communication. Your tone of voice can convey your emotions, intentions, and attitudes, influencing how your message is perceived by others. By speaking in a calm and respectful manner, you can foster trust, openness, and understanding in your interactions with others. Similarly, your body language can communicate a great deal about your emotions and intentions, so it is important to pay attention to your posture, gestures, and facial expressions when communicating with others.

In addition to these components, it is important to consider the context and purpose of your communication when developing effective ways to communicate with others. Understanding the specific needs, preferences, and expectations of your audience can help you tailor your message to effectively convey your ideas and goals. Whether you are giving a presentation to colleagues, having a difficult conversation with a friend, or negotiating with a client, being mindful of the context and purpose of your communication can help you communicate more effectively and achieve better outcomes.

Effective communication is a skill that can be developed and improved over time with practice and self-awareness. By actively listening to others, speaking clearly and concisely, being mindful of your tone of voice and body language, and considering the context and purpose of your communication, you can enhance your ability to connect with others, build strong relationships, and achieve your goals. In the next section, we will provide practical tips and strategies to help you improve your communication skills and develop effective ways to communicate with others in various settings.

- Practicing active listening and body language cues

Active listening is a crucial skill in effective communication that involves not only hearing the words spoken by a speaker but also actively engaging with the content and emotions behind those words. By practicing active listening, individuals can demonstrate their interest and understanding of the speaker's message, which can lead to stronger connections and more productive conversations. One key aspect of active listening is the use of body language cues to show attentiveness and empathy towards the speaker. Body language plays a significant role in communication, as it can convey a plethora of emotions and intentions without saying a word. By being mindful of our body language cues, we can create a more supportive and engaging environment for the speaker, ultimately leading to more meaningful interactions.

When practicing active listening, it is essential to be fully present and engaged in the conversation. This means setting aside distractions, such as phones or other devices, and focusing on the speaker and their message. By giving the speaker your full attention, you are showing them respect and signaling that their words are important to you. Additionally, maintaining eye contact with the speaker can convey sincerity and interest in what they have to say. Eye contact is a powerful nonverbal cue that can help establish trust and connection between individuals, making the speaker feel heard and valued.

Another important aspect of active listening is to provide verbal and nonverbal feedback to the speaker to demonstrate understanding and encourage further communication. Verbal cues such as nodding, saying "mm-hmm" or "I see," can indicate that you are actively listening and processing the speaker's message. Nonverbal cues, such as smiling, leaning forward slightly, or mirroring the speaker's body language, can also convey openness and receptiveness to what is being said. By providing both verbal and nonverbal feedback, you are letting the speaker know that you are engaged and interested in their perspective, which can help build rapport and trust in the conversation.

In addition to providing feedback, it is crucial to ask clarifying questions and paraphrase the speaker's message to ensure that you have understood their point correctly. Asking open-ended questions can encourage the speaker to elaborate on their thoughts and feelings, leading to a deeper and more meaningful conversation. Paraphrasing the speaker's message back to them in your own words can help confirm your understanding and show that you are actively listening and trying to comprehend their perspective. By asking questions and paraphrasing, you are demonstrating your commitment to understanding the speaker's message and creating a supportive environment for effective communication.

Furthermore, being mindful of your own body language cues can have a significant impact on the success of active listening. Avoiding negative body language, such as crossing arms, fidgeting, or avoiding eye contact, can signal disinterest or defensiveness to the speaker. Instead, maintain an open posture, face the speaker directly, and use gestures and facial expressions to convey empathy and understanding. By aligning your body language with your verbal cues, you can create a more cohesive and supportive environment for communication, enhancing the effectiveness of active listening. By actively listening to the speaker, providing feedback, asking clarifying questions, and being mindful of your own body language, you can create a more supportive and engaging environment for productive conversations. By demonstrating attentiveness and empathy through active listening and positive body language cues, you can build stronger connections, foster trust, and enhance the quality of your interactions with others. Make a conscious effort to practice active listening and be aware of your body language cues in your daily interactions, and you will see a positive impact on your communication skills and relationships.

Chapter 4: Making Friends

- TIPS ON HOW TO INITIATE friendships and maintain connections

Building and maintaining friendships is an essential aspect of human relationships that can bring joy, support, and fulfillment to our lives. However, for many people, initiating friendships and maintaining connections can be a daunting task. In this article, we will explore some tips and strategies to help you navigate the complexities of forming and sustaining meaningful friendships.

One of the first steps in initiating friendships is to be open and approachable. Being friendly and welcoming to others can create an inviting atmosphere that encourages people to engage with you. Smile, make eye contact, and show genuine interest in others by asking questions and listening attentively. By demonstrating warmth and friendliness, you can make it easier for others to approach you and initiate conversations.

Another important tip for initiating friendships is to be proactive in seeking out opportunities to meet new people. Join clubs, groups, or organizations that align with your interests and passions. Attend social events, gatherings, or networking functions where you can interact with a diverse range of individuals. By putting yourself in social situations, you increase the likelihood of meeting like-minded people who share your values and hobbies.

It is also important to be authentic and genuine in your interactions with others. Be yourself and let your true personality shine through. Authenticity is key to building trust and establishing meaningful connections with others. Avoid trying to impress or pretend to be someone you are not. Instead, focus on being honest, sincere, and vulnerable in your conversations. Show your true self and let others see the real you.

In addition to being open, approachable, proactive, and authentic, it is crucial to be a good listener in initiating friendships. Listening is a fundamental skill that can help you connect with others on a deeper level. Show empathy, respect, and understanding towards others by actively listening to their thoughts, feelings, and experiences. Ask open-ended questions and encourage others to share their stories and insights. By showing attentiveness and empathy, you can foster a sense of trust and rapport in your interactions.

Once you have initiated a friendship, it is important to make an effort to maintain and nurture the connection over time. Building and sustaining friendships require ongoing effort, communication, and commitment. Stay in touch with your friends regularly by reaching out through phone calls, text messages, emails, or social media. Make plans to meet up for coffee, lunch, or other activities to maintain the connection and strengthen the bond.

Another important aspect of maintaining friendships is showing appreciation and gratitude towards your friends. Acknowledge their efforts, support, and presence in your life by expressing your gratitude and thankfulness. Celebrate their achievements, milestones, and successes, and offer support and encouragement during challenging times. By showing appreciation and gratitude, you can reinforce the value of the friendship and deepen the emotional connection.

Additionally, it is essential to be a good friend by being there for others when they need you. Offer your support, assistance, and encouragement to your friends when they are facing challenges, setbacks, or difficulties. Listen attentively to their concerns, provide a shoulder to lean on, and offer practical help or advice when needed. Be reliable, trustworthy, and dependable in your friendships by honoring your commitments and respecting boundaries.

Furthermore, it is crucial to communicate openly and honestly with your friends to maintain healthy and thriving relationships. Address any conflicts, misunderstandings, or issues that may arise in a respectful and constructive manner. Be willing to have difficult conversations, express your thoughts and feelings openly, and listen to the perspectives of your friends with an open mind. By fostering clear and honest communication, you can strengthen the trust, understanding, and harmony in your friendships. By being open, approachable, proactive, authentic, and empathetic, you can create opportunities to meet new people, form meaningful connections, and build lasting friendships. Show appreciation, gratitude, and support towards your friends, and be there for them when they need you. Communicate openly, honestly, and respectfully to address any conflicts or issues that may arise. By following these tips and strategies, you can cultivate strong, healthy, and fulfilling friendships that enrich your life and bring joy and companionship to your journey.

- Overcoming social anxiety in group settings

Social anxiety is a common mental health issue that affects many individuals in group settings. It can be challenging to navigate social interactions and feel comfortable in large groups, leading to feelings of fear, self-consciousness, and insecurity. However, there are several strategies that can help individuals overcome social anxiety and feel more at ease in group settings.

One effective strategy for overcoming social anxiety in group settings is to practice mindfulness and relaxation techniques. By focusing on the present moment and calming the mind, individuals can reduce feelings of anxiety and better cope with social interactions. Breathing exercises, visualization techniques, and progressive muscle relaxation can all help individuals calm their nerves and approach social situations with a sense of calm and confidence.

Another helpful strategy for overcoming social anxiety in group settings is to challenge negative thoughts and beliefs. Many individuals with social anxiety have irrational fears and beliefs that contribute to their anxiety. By identifying and challenging these negative thoughts, individuals can develop more realistic and positive beliefs about themselves and their social interactions. Cognitive-behavioral therapy (CBT) is a highly effective approach for identifying and changing negative thought patterns, and can help individuals challenge their fears and develop healthier coping strategies.

In addition to mindfulness and cognitive-behavioral techniques, individuals can also benefit from gradual exposure to social situations. By gradually exposing themselves to group settings and practicing social interactions, individuals can desensitize themselves to the fear and anxiety they experience. This can help individuals build confidence and develop social skills, making it easier to navigate group settings in the future. It is important for individuals to start small and gradually increase the difficulty of social situations they expose themselves to, in order to build confidence and reduce anxiety.

Social support can also play a critical role in helping individuals overcome social anxiety in group settings. By surrounding themselves with supportive friends and family members, individuals can feel more comfortable and confident in social situations. Having a support network can provide reassurance, encouragement, and a sense of belonging, which can help individuals cope with their anxiety and feel more at ease in group settings. Supportive relationships can provide a sense of security and acceptance, which can help individuals feel more confident and less anxious in social situations.

It is important for individuals to remember that overcoming social anxiety is a gradual process that takes time and effort. It is normal to experience setbacks and challenges along the way, but with persistence and determination, individuals can learn to manage their anxiety and feel more comfortable in group settings. By practicing mindfulness techniques, challenging negative thoughts, gradually exposing themselves to social situations, and seeking social support, individuals can develop the skills and confidence needed to overcome social anxiety and thrive in group settings. With the right strategies and support, individuals can learn to navigate social interactions with ease and confidence, leading to improved mental health and overall well-being.

Chapter 5: Conflict Resolution

- TEACHING CHILDREN conflict resolution skills

Conflict resolution skills are essential tools that children need to navigate the complexities of social interactions both in and out of school. It is important for children to learn how to effectively manage conflicts and find peaceful resolutions in order to build healthy relationships and develop strong emotional intelligence. By teaching children conflict resolution skills, we are empowering them to communicate effectively, empathize with others, and collaborate towards finding mutually satisfying solutions.

One important aspect of teaching children conflict resolution skills is helping them understand the different types of conflicts that can arise. Children need to recognize that conflict is a natural part of human relationships and that it is normal to have differing opinions or perspectives. By understanding that conflicts can be either relational, task-focused, or value-based, children can better identify the root of the conflict and choose appropriate strategies to resolve it. Teaching children to differentiate between constructive and destructive conflicts can also help them approach conflicts in a positive and productive manner.

Another crucial component of teaching children conflict resolution skills is helping them develop effective communication skills. Children need to learn how to express their thoughts, feelings, and needs clearly and assertively, while also listening actively to others and seeking to understand their perspectives. By teaching children the importance of using "I" statements, active listening, and nonverbal communication cues, we can equip them with the tools they need to communicate effectively during conflicts and work towards finding solutions that benefit everyone involved.

Empathy is another key element of conflict resolution skills that children need to develop. Teaching children to empathize with others means helping them understand and validate the feelings and perspectives of those involved in the conflict. By encouraging children to consider the thoughts and emotions of others, we can help them cultivate compassion, respect, and understanding, which are essential for fostering positive and empathetic relationships. Through activities such as role-playing, storytelling, and discussions about feelings, we can help children develop their empathy skills and learn to approach conflicts with compassion and empathy.

Teaching children conflict resolution skills also involves helping them develop problem-solving and negotiation skills. Children need to learn how to analyze the different options available to them, propose creative and fair solutions, and negotiate effectively with others to reach a mutually satisfying outcome. By teaching children the importance of brainstorming, compromising, and collaborating with others, we can empower them to take an active role in resolving conflicts and finding solutions that meet the needs of all parties involved. Through practice and guidance, children can develop their problem-solving and negotiation skills and become confident in their ability to handle conflicts constructively.

It is important for educators and parents to create a supportive and inclusive environment where children can practice and apply their conflict resolution skills. By setting clear expectations for respectful communication, modeling positive conflict resolution strategies, and providing opportunities for children to practice their skills through role-playing, group discussions, and real-life scenarios, we can help them build confidence and proficiency in managing conflicts. It is also important to provide feedback, encouragement, and reinforcement to children as they navigate conflicts and work towards finding peaceful resolutions. By creating a culture of respect, empathy, and collaboration, we can empower children to become confident and capable problem solvers who can navigate conflicts effectively and build harmonious relationships with others. By equipping children with the tools they need to communicate effectively, empathize with others, and problem-solve collaboratively, we are preparing them to navigate conflicts in a positive and constructive manner. Through guidance, practice, and support, children can develop their conflict resolution skills and build the foundation for healthy and successful relationships both in childhood and in the future. By empowering children to approach conflicts with empathy, respect, and creativity, we are helping them become confident and compassionate individuals who can contribute positively to their communities and society as a whole.

- Strategies for dealing with disagreements and misunderstandings

Disagreements and misunderstandings are common occurrences in both personal and professional relationships. These conflicts can arise from differences in opinions, values, or communication styles. It is important to have effective strategies in place to address disagreements and misunderstandings in a constructive and respectful manner. In this article, we will explore some key strategies for dealing with disagreements and misunderstandings in various contexts.

One of the most important strategies for dealing with disagreements and misunderstandings is effective communication. Communication lies at the heart of resolving conflicts, as it enables individuals to express their thoughts and feelings, listen to others' perspectives, and work towards finding common ground. When faced with a disagreement or misunderstanding, it is essential to engage in open and honest communication with the other party. This involves actively listening to their concerns, asking clarifying questions, and expressing your own thoughts and feelings in a clear and respectful manner. By fostering open communication, individuals can gain a deeper understanding of each other's perspectives and work towards finding a mutually acceptable solution.

Another key strategy for addressing disagreements and misunderstandings is to focus on finding common ground. While individuals may have different opinions or viewpoints, there are often shared goals or values that can serve as a basis for agreement. By identifying common ground, individuals can work together to find solutions that are mutually beneficial and address the underlying issues of the disagreement. This can involve exploring areas of agreement, acknowledging the validity of each other's perspectives, and seeking compromise where necessary. By focusing on common ground, individuals can foster a collaborative approach to resolving conflicts and moving forward in a positive direction.

In addition to effective communication and finding common ground, it is important to manage emotions when dealing with disagreements and misunderstandings. Conflicts can evoke strong emotions such as anger, frustration, or hurt, which can cloud judgment and hinder the resolution process. It is crucial to recognize and acknowledge these emotions, while also maintaining a sense of calm and composure. Individuals can practice self-awareness techniques, such as deep breathing or taking a break, to regulate their emotions and approach the conflict with a clear and rational mindset. By managing emotions effectively, individuals can prevent conflicts from escalating and work towards finding a productive resolution.

Furthermore, seeking a third-party perspective can be a helpful strategy for addressing disagreements and misunderstandings. In some cases, conflicts may be difficult to resolve between the involved parties alone. In such situations, it can be beneficial to seek the input of a neutral third party, such as a mediator or a trusted colleague. A third party can provide an unbiased perspective on the conflict, facilitate communication between the parties, and help guide the resolution process in a fair and impartial manner. By involving a third party, individuals can gain new insights into the conflict, explore alternative solutions, and work towards a resolution that is mutually acceptable to all parties involved.

Lastly, it is important to learn from disagreements and misunderstandings in order to prevent future conflicts. Conflict resolution is a skill that can be developed and honed over time through practice and reflection. Individuals can evaluate past conflicts, identify patterns or triggers that led to disagreements, and learn from their mistakes to improve their conflict resolution skills in the future. By reflecting on past conflicts and engaging in continuous self-improvement, individuals can build stronger relationships, enhance their communication skills, and navigate conflicts more effectively in the long run. By fostering open communication, finding common ground, managing emotions, seeking third-party perspectives, and learning from conflicts, individuals can address disagreements and misunderstandings in a constructive and respectful manner. Conflict resolution is a valuable skill that can benefit individuals in various aspects of their personal and professional lives. By developing effective conflict resolution strategies, individuals can build stronger relationships, enhance their communication skills, and work towards finding mutually acceptable solutions to conflicts.

Chapter 6: Empathy and Understanding Others

- ENCOURAGING EMPATHY and understanding in children

Encouraging empathy and understanding in children is a crucial aspect of their development and overall well-being. Empathy is the ability to understand and share the feelings of others, while understanding refers to the ability to comprehend someone else's perspective, beliefs, and emotions. These skills are essential for healthy relationships, effective communication, and moral reasoning. Research has shown that children who display higher levels of empathy and understanding have better social skills, are more successful in school, and experience less aggression and conflict in their interactions with others.

One way to encourage empathy and understanding in children is through modeling these behaviors in our own actions and interactions. Children learn by observing the behavior of adults, so it is important to demonstrate empathy and understanding in our daily lives. This can involve actively listening to others, expressing empathy for their feelings, and trying to see things from their perspective. By modeling these behaviors, we can help children learn how to empathize with others and understand different points of view.

Another important way to encourage empathy and understanding in children is through storytelling and literature. Reading and discussing books that feature characters from diverse backgrounds and experiences can help children develop empathy and understanding for people who are different from themselves. By exploring different perspectives and emotions through literature, children can learn to appreciate the diversity of human experiences and develop a more empathetic and understanding mindset.

In addition to modeling and storytelling, teaching children about emotions and how to cope with them can also help promote empathy and understanding. By helping children identify and understand their own emotions, we can teach them to recognize and empathize with the feelings of others. This can involve discussing different emotions, practicing emotional regulation techniques, and encouraging children to express their feelings in a healthy and constructive way. By fostering emotional intelligence in children, we can help them develop a greater sense of empathy and understanding for others.

Furthermore, promoting empathy and understanding in children can also involve teaching them about the value of kindness, compassion, and respect. By emphasizing the importance of treating others with empathy and understanding, we can help children cultivate a sense of empathy and compassion for those around them. This can involve discussing the impact of our words and actions on others, practicing acts of kindness and generosity, and encouraging children to consider the feelings and perspectives of others before acting. By instilling these values in children, we can help them develop a deeper understanding and appreciation for the experiences and emotions of others. By modeling empathetic behavior, exploring diverse perspectives through literature, teaching children about emotions, and promoting kindness and compassion, we can help children cultivate a greater sense of empathy and understanding for others. These skills are essential for building strong, healthy relationships, effective communication, and moral reasoning in children, and can have a lasting impact on their social and emotional development. By prioritizing empathy and understanding in our interactions with children, we can help them become more empathetic, caring, and compassionate individuals who contribute positively to their communities and the world at large.

- Recognizing emotional cues and perspectives of others

Recognizing emotional cues and perspectives of others is a crucial skill in both personal and professional settings. It involves being able to understand and identify the emotions and perspectives of those around us, and respond appropriately in order to build effective relationships and facilitate positive interactions. This skill is often referred to as emotional intelligence, which encompasses the ability to recognize, understand, and manage our own emotions, as well as the emotions of others.

One key aspect of recognizing emotional cues and perspectives of others is being able to accurately identify and interpret nonverbal cues such as facial expressions, body language, and tone of voice. These cues can provide valuable insights into a person's emotional state and help us better understand their perspectives and motivations. For example, a furrowed brow and clenched fists may indicate anger or frustration, while a relaxed posture and smile may signal happiness or contentment.

Another important element of recognizing emotional cues and perspectives is actively listening to others and practicing empathy. By listening attentively and trying to put ourselves in the other person's shoes, we can gain a better understanding of their emotions and perspectives. This can help us respond appropriately and effectively, whether we are providing support to a friend in need or negotiating in a professional setting.

In addition to nonverbal cues and empathetic listening, recognizing emotional cues and perspectives of others also involves being aware of cultural differences and individual differences in emotional expression. Different cultures may have varying norms and preferences when it comes to expressing emotions, so it is important to be sensitive to these differences and adapt our communication style accordingly. Furthermore, individuals may vary in their emotional sensitivity and how they express their emotions, so it is important to take these differences into account when interacting with others. By honing this skill, we can improve our communication and interpersonal relationships, foster greater understanding and collaboration, and create more positive and harmonious environments both personally and professionally. Practicing emotional intelligence can lead to increased empathy, trust, and emotional connection with others, ultimately contributing to a more fulfilling and enriching life.

Chapter 7: Social Etiquette

- LEARNING MANNERS AND etiquette in social settings

Manners and etiquette play a crucial role in how we interact with others in social settings. These codes of behavior help ensure that our interactions are respectful, polite, and considerate. Learning and practicing good manners can go a long way in making a positive impression on others and building strong relationships. In today's fast-paced and technology-driven world, the importance of manners and etiquette may sometimes be overlooked or taken for granted. However, they remain essential skills that can greatly enhance our social interactions and contribute to our overall success and well-being.

One of the key aspects of manners and etiquette is the way we communicate with others. This includes not only what we say but also how we say it. Politeness, respect, and consideration should always be at the forefront of our interactions. This means speaking politely, using proper language, and being mindful of our tone and body language. It also means listening actively and attentively to others, showing interest in what they have to say, and refraining from interrupting or dominating the conversation. By following these basic principles of communication, we can show others that we value and respect them, leading to more positive and meaningful interactions.

Another important aspect of manners and etiquette is how we behave in various social settings. This includes being punctual, dressing appropriately, and adhering to the social norms of the particular setting. For example, at a formal event such as a wedding or a business meeting, it is important to dress in appropriate attire and conduct oneself with professionalism and decorum. On the other hand, in a more casual setting such as a social gathering with friends, it is still important to show respect and consideration for others by being polite, friendly, and engaging.

Good manners and etiquette also extend to how we treat others in social settings. This includes being kind, considerate, and empathetic towards others. It means showing appreciation for others' efforts, acknowledging their contributions, and expressing gratitude for their presence. It also means being inclusive and considerate of others' feelings, opinions, and preferences. By demonstrating kindness and empathy towards others, we can create a positive and harmonious atmosphere in social settings, leading to stronger and more fulfilling relationships.

In addition to these basic principles of manners and etiquette, there are also specific customs and traditions that may vary depending on the cultural context. For example, different cultures may have different expectations regarding greetings, gestures, and forms of address. It is important to be aware of and respectful towards these cultural norms when interacting with individuals from different backgrounds. By showing an awareness and appreciation of cultural differences, we can demonstrate our openness, tolerance, and respect for diversity, fostering more inclusive and harmonious social interactions. By communicating politely, behaving respectfully, treating others kindly, and being aware of cultural differences, we can create a positive and harmonious atmosphere in social settings. These basic principles of communication and behavior can help us show respect, consideration, and empathy towards others, leading to stronger and more fulfilling relationships. In today's complex and interconnected world, the ability to navigate social situations with grace and tact is a valuable skill that can contribute to our success and well-being. Let us strive to cultivate good manners and etiquette in our interactions and create a more respectful and compassionate society.

- Understanding the importance of respect and politeness

Respect and politeness are fundamental aspects of human interaction that play a crucial role in shaping relationships and maintaining social harmony. These values are deeply ingrained in societal norms and etiquette, serving as guiding principles that promote civility, empathy, and understanding among individuals. Respect is defined as a feeling of deep admiration for someone or something based on their qualities, achievements, or abilities. In the context of interpersonal relationships, respect is demonstrated through courteous behavior, consideration for others' feelings, and acknowledgment of their perspectives. On the other hand, politeness refers to the use of manners, etiquette, and social conventions to show respect and consideration towards others.

The importance of respect and politeness in interpersonal communication cannot be overstated. When individuals treat each other with respect and courtesy, they create a positive and harmonious atmosphere that fosters trust, cooperation, and mutual understanding. In contrast, a lack of respect and politeness can lead to misunderstandings, conflicts, and breakdowns in communication. By cultivating a culture of respect and politeness, individuals can build strong and meaningful relationships that are characterized by mutual trust, empathy, and cooperation.

Respect and politeness are essential in the workplace as well, where they play a significant role in shaping organizational culture, employee morale, and overall productivity. When colleagues, supervisors, and subordinates treat each other with respect and courtesy, they create a supportive and positive work environment that fosters teamwork, collaboration, and innovation. In contrast, a work environment marked by disrespect, rudeness, or hostility can lead to employee dissatisfaction, low morale, and diminished productivity. By promoting a culture of respect and politeness in the workplace, organizations can enhance employee engagement, retention, and job satisfaction.

Respect and politeness are also critical in the context of diversity and inclusion, where they serve as the foundation for building a culture of tolerance, acceptance, and equality. In a diverse society, individuals come from various cultural backgrounds, beliefs, and perspectives, making it essential to treat each other with respect and courtesy. By showing respect for others' differences, individuals can foster a sense of inclusivity, belonging, and acceptance, creating a more equitable and harmonious society. In contrast, a lack of respect and politeness can lead to discrimination, prejudice, and alienation, perpetuating social divisions and inequalities. By promoting respect and politeness in interactions with people from diverse backgrounds, individuals can contribute to building a more inclusive and harmonious society. By treating each other with respect and courtesy, individuals can create a positive and supportive atmosphere that enhances communication, trust, and cooperation. Whether in personal relationships, the workplace, or society at large, respect and politeness are fundamental principles that guide interactions and promote understanding and empathy among individuals. By upholding these values in daily interactions, individuals can contribute to building a more respectful, inclusive, and harmonious world for all.

Chapter 8: Dealing with Bullying

- IDENTIFYING DIFFERENT types of bullying and its effects

Bullying is a pervasive issue that affects individuals of all ages and backgrounds. It is a form of aggressive behavior that is intentional, repetitive, and involves a power imbalance between the bully and the victim. There are several different types of bullying, each with its own unique characteristics and effects on the individuals involved.

One of the most common types of bullying is verbal bullying. This involves using words to hurt, intimidate, or humiliate the victim. Verbal bullying can take many forms, including name-calling, teasing, insults, threats, and spreading rumors. This type of bullying can have a significant impact on the victim's self-esteem and mental health. It can lead to feelings of shame, embarrassment, and worthlessness, as well as feelings of fear and anxiety.

Another common type of bullying is physical bullying. This involves using physical force or aggression to harm the victim. Physical bullying can include hitting, kicking, punching, pushing, and other forms of physical violence. This type of bullying can cause physical injuries, as well as emotional trauma. Victims of physical bullying may experience pain, fear, and a sense of helplessness. They may also develop feelings of anger, resentment, and a desire for revenge.

Cyberbullying is a modern form of bullying that takes place online or through electronic devices. This can include sending threatening or harassing messages, spreading rumors or lies, posting embarrassing photos or videos, and other forms of online abuse. Cyberbullying can have a profound impact on the victim's mental health and well-being. It can lead to feelings of isolation, depression, and anxiety. Victims of cyberbullying may also experience social withdrawal, decreased self-esteem, and even thoughts of self-harm or suicide.

In addition to these main types of bullying, there are also various subtypes of bullying that can occur in different settings. For example, workplace bullying involves harassment or mistreatment of an employee by a supervisor or coworker. This can include verbal abuse, threats, intimidation, and sabotage. Workplace bullying can have serious consequences for the victim, including job insecurity, decreased job satisfaction, and poor mental health.

Another subtype of bullying is sexual bullying, which involves unwanted sexual behavior or comments that are intended to humiliate or degrade the victim. This can include sexual harassment, sexual assault, and other forms of sexual misconduct. Sexual bullying can have a devastating impact on the victim's emotional and psychological well-being. It can lead to feelings of shame, guilt, and powerlessness, as well as long-term trauma and post-traumatic stress disorder.

Regardless of the type of bullying, it is important to recognize the effects that it can have on individuals. Victims of bullying may experience a range of physical, emotional, and psychological symptoms. These can include anxiety, depression, low self-esteem, suicidal thoughts, and even physical health problems. In some cases, the effects of bullying can be long-lasting and have a significant impact on the individual's overall well-being.

It is essential to address bullying and its effects in a comprehensive and proactive manner. This includes implementing strategies to prevent bullying from occurring, as well as providing support and resources for individuals who have experienced bullying. Educating individuals about the different types of bullying and its effects is a crucial step in raising awareness and promoting a culture of respect and kindness. By working together to combat bullying, we can create safer and more inclusive communities for everyone.

- Strategies for handling and preventing bullying situations

Bullying is a pervasive issue that affects individuals of all ages and backgrounds. It can have serious consequences for the physical, emotional, and psychological well-being of those involved. In order to effectively address and prevent bullying, it is important to understand the underlying causes and dynamics of bullying behavior. By implementing strategic approaches and interventions, educators, parents, and community members can work together to create a safe and supportive environment for all individuals.

One key strategy for handling and preventing bullying situations is to promote empathy and communication skills among students. Research has shown that individuals who engage in bullying behavior often lack the ability to empathize with others and may struggle with effective communication. By teaching students to understand and consider the feelings and perspectives of their peers, we can help cultivate a culture of respect and empathy within schools and communities. Encouraging open and honest communication can also empower students to speak up and seek help when they witness or experience bullying behavior.

Another important strategy for addressing bullying situations is to implement clear policies and procedures for addressing incidents of bullying. Schools and organizations should have comprehensive anti-bullying policies in place that outline expectations for behavior and consequences for those who engage in bullying behavior. These policies should be communicated clearly to students, parents, and staff members to ensure that everyone understands their role in preventing and addressing bullying. Additionally, it is essential to provide training and support for educators and administrators on how to effectively respond to reports of bullying and support those who have been impacted by bullying.

In addition to promoting empathy and communication skills and implementing clear policies and procedures, it is crucial to actively engage students in bullying prevention efforts. By involving students in the development and implementation of anti-bullying initiatives, we can empower them to take ownership of creating a positive and inclusive school culture. Students can play a key role in promoting kindness, empathy, and respect among their peers, and can serve as leaders in addressing and preventing bullying behavior. By providing students with opportunities to participate in awareness campaigns, peer support programs, and student-led initiatives, we can foster a sense of community and unity that rejects bullying and promotes positive social interactions.

Furthermore, collaboration between schools, families, and community organizations is essential for effectively addressing and preventing bullying situations. Parents and caregivers play a critical role in supporting their children and advocating for their safety and well-being. By establishing open lines of communication between parents, educators, and community partners, we can work together to address the root causes of bullying and create a network of support for those who have been impacted by bullying. Community organizations can also play a key role in providing resources and support for bullying prevention efforts, such as mental health services, counseling, and educational programs. By working together to create a culture of respect, empathy, and inclusivity, we can create safe and supportive environments where all individuals can thrive. Together, we can make a difference in the lives of those affected by bullying and create a future free from harassment and intimidation.

Chapter 9: Building Positive Relationships

- NURTURING POSITIVE relationships with peers and adults

Nurturing positive relationships with peers and adults is essential for personal and professional growth. Research has shown that individuals who have strong social connections are happier, healthier, and more successful in various aspects of their lives. Positive relationships with both peers and adults provide support, encouragement, and a sense of belonging that can help individuals navigate life's challenges and achieve their goals. In this article, we will explore the importance of nurturing positive relationships with peers and adults, as well as provide practical strategies for building and maintaining these connections.

Peer relationships play a crucial role in our development, especially during adolescence when peers become increasingly influential. Positive peer relationships can provide emotional support, companionship, and a sense of belonging that is essential for overall well-being. These relationships can also help individuals develop important social skills such as communication, conflict resolution, and empathy. By fostering positive relationships with peers, individuals can create a supportive network that can help them navigate the ups and downs of life.

Similarly, positive relationships with adults, such as teachers, mentors, and supervisors, are also important for personal and professional growth. Adults can provide guidance, advice, and opportunities for learning and development that can help individuals reach their full potential. These relationships can also offer valuable insights and perspectives that individuals may not have considered on their own. By nurturing positive relationships with adults, individuals can gain valuable support and mentorship that can help them achieve their goals and advance in their careers.

Building and maintaining positive relationships with peers and adults requires time, effort, and genuine interest in the well-being of others. One important strategy for nurturing these relationships is active listening. By taking the time to listen to others and show genuine interest in their thoughts and feelings, individuals can build trust and rapport that can lay the foundation for a strong relationship. Active listening involves not only hearing what others have to say but also showing empathy and understanding towards their perspective.

Another key strategy for nurturing positive relationships with peers and adults is effective communication. Clear and respectful communication is essential for building trust and resolving conflicts that may arise in relationships. By expressing thoughts and feelings honestly and respectfully, individuals can foster open and honest communication that can strengthen their relationships with others. It is also important to practice good communication skills such as giving and receiving feedback, asking for clarification when needed, and expressing appreciation for others.

In addition to active listening and effective communication, showing empathy and understanding towards others is crucial for nurturing positive relationships with peers and adults. Empathy involves putting oneself in the shoes of others and understanding their thoughts, feelings, and perspectives. By showing empathy towards others, individuals can build trust and deepen their connections with others. It is important to show empathy towards others even when disagreements arise, as it can help individuals navigate conflicts and find common ground.

It is also important to be supportive and encouraging towards others in order to nurture positive relationships with peers and adults. Providing emotional support, encouragement, and praise to others can help strengthen their self-esteem and confidence. By being a source of support and encouragement for others, individuals can create a positive and nurturing environment that fosters growth and development. It is important to be there for others in times of need, listen to their concerns, and offer help and advice when needed. By building strong connections with others, individuals can gain support, guidance, and opportunities for learning and development that can help them achieve their goals and reach their full potential. By practicing active listening, effective communication, empathy, and support towards others, individuals can create a positive and nurturing environment that fosters strong and meaningful relationships. By investing time and effort into building and maintaining positive relationships with peers and adults, individuals can reap the benefits of a supportive network that can help them navigate life's challenges and achieve success.

- Recognizing the qualities of healthy friendships

In order to fully grasp the qualities of healthy friendships, it is important to understand the underlying principles that contribute to their success. Healthy friendships are characterized by mutual respect, trust, empathy, and support. These qualities form the foundation of a strong and lasting friendship that can withstand the test of time and adversity.

One of the key qualities of healthy friendships is mutual respect. This means that both parties value and acknowledge each other's opinions, beliefs, and boundaries. Respect allows for open and honest communication, where both friends feel heard and understood. It also ensures that both parties are treated with kindness and consideration, even in moments of disagreement or conflict.

Trust is another essential quality of healthy friendships. Trust involves being able to rely on and confide in each other without fear of judgment or betrayal. Trust is built over time through consistent honesty, reliability, and loyalty. When friends trust each other, they are able to share their thoughts, feelings, and experiences without reservation, knowing that their confidences will be kept safe.

Empathy is a crucial component of healthy friendships as well. Empathy is the ability to understand and share in the feelings of another person. Friends who demonstrate empathy are able to offer support, comfort, and understanding during both happy and challenging times. Empathy allows friends to connect on a deeper level, fostering a strong emotional bond that enhances the quality of the friendship.

Support is another key quality of healthy friendships. Friends who support each other offer encouragement, guidance, and assistance when needed. They celebrate each other's successes and provide comfort and reassurance in times of difficulty. Supportive friends show up for each other, offer a listening ear, and provide a shoulder to lean on when needed. This sense of solidarity and companionship strengthens the bond between friends and creates a sense of security and belonging.

In addition to these core qualities, healthy friendships are characterized by open communication, shared interests, and a sense of mutual growth and development. Communication is vital in any relationship, as it allows friends to express their thoughts, feelings, and needs openly and honestly. When friends communicate effectively, they are able to resolve conflicts, deepen their connection, and strengthen their friendship.

Shared interests and activities play a crucial role in healthy friendships as well. Friends who share common hobbies, values, and goals are able to bond over their mutual interests and create meaningful experiences together. These shared experiences help to strengthen the friendship and create lasting memories that deepen the connection between friends.

Furthermore, healthy friendships are characterized by a sense of mutual growth and development. Friends who support each other's personal growth and success are able to thrive together and create a positive impact on each other's lives. They encourage each other to reach their full potential, pursue their dreams, and overcome challenges with resilience and determination.

Ultimately, recognizing the qualities of healthy friendships requires a combination of self-awareness, communication skills, empathy, and a commitment to mutual respect and support. By cultivating these qualities in our friendships, we can create strong and lasting bonds that enrich our lives and bring us joy, fulfillment, and support in both good times and bad.

Chapter 10: Overcoming Social Anxiety

- TECHNIQUES TO MANAGE social anxiety and nervousness

Social anxiety and nervousness are common experiences that many individuals face in their daily lives. These feelings can arise in various social situations, such as giving a presentation, meeting new people, or attending social events. While it is normal to feel anxious or nervous at times, excessive social anxiety can significantly impact an individual's quality of life and hinder their ability to effectively engage with others. Fortunately, there are techniques that can help manage social anxiety and nervousness, allowing individuals to feel more confident and comfortable in social situations.

One effective technique for managing social anxiety and nervousness is deep breathing exercises. Deep breathing can help calm the body's physiological response to anxiety by activating the parasympathetic nervous system, which is responsible for relaxation. By taking slow, deep breaths and focusing on the inhalation and exhalation, individuals can reduce feelings of anxiety and stress. Deep breathing exercises can be done discreetly in any social situation, making them a convenient and accessible tool for managing social anxiety.

Another technique that can help manage social anxiety and nervousness is cognitive restructuring. Cognitive restructuring involves identifying and challenging negative thought patterns that contribute to anxiety and replacing them with more positive and realistic thoughts. For example, if an individual is nervous about speaking in front of a group because they fear making a mistake, they can challenge this thought by reminding themselves that it is natural to make mistakes and that it does not define their worth as a person. By reframing negative thoughts in a more positive light, individuals can reduce their anxiety and build their confidence in social situations.

Behavioral techniques, such as exposure therapy, can also be effective in managing social anxiety and nervousness. Exposure therapy involves gradually exposing oneself to anxiety-provoking situations in a controlled and systematic manner. By repeatedly facing their fears and learning to tolerate discomfort, individuals can desensitize themselves to social anxiety triggers and build their confidence in social settings. For example, someone who is anxious about attending social events could start by attending small gatherings with close friends before gradually working up to larger events with unfamiliar people. Over time, exposure therapy can help individuals confront their fears and develop coping strategies to manage their social anxiety.

Mindfulness techniques can also be helpful in managing social anxiety and nervousness. Mindfulness involves bringing one's attention to the present moment without judgment or attachment to thoughts or emotions. By practicing mindfulness, individuals can learn to observe their anxious thoughts and physical sensations without becoming overwhelmed by them. Mindfulness techniques, such as meditation or body scanning, can help individuals stay grounded and focused in social situations, reducing their reactivity to anxiety triggers. By cultivating a sense of mindfulness, individuals can develop greater self-awareness and emotional regulation, making it easier to navigate social interactions with confidence and poise.

In addition to these techniques, social skills training can be beneficial for individuals struggling with social anxiety and nervousness. Social skills training involves learning and practicing effective communication, assertiveness, and interpersonal skills to navigate social interactions more confidently. By acquiring these skills, individuals can feel more prepared and competent in various social situations, reducing their anxiety and improving their overall social functioning. Social skills training can be especially helpful for individuals who struggle with social anxiety due to a lack of experience or confidence in social settings, providing them with practical tools and strategies to enhance their social interactions.

It is important to recognize that managing social anxiety and nervousness is a gradual process that requires patience and persistence. Individuals may not see immediate results from implementing these techniques, but with consistent practice and self-care, they can gradually build their confidence and reduce their anxiety in social situations. Seeking support from a mental health professional or joining a support group can also be beneficial for individuals struggling with social anxiety, providing them with guidance, encouragement, and validation as they work towards managing their anxiety. By incorporating these techniques and seeking support, individuals can learn to navigate social situations with greater ease and confidence, ultimately improving their quality of life and well-being.

- Building resilience in social situations

Building resilience in social situations is a crucial skill that can greatly enhance one's overall well-being and success in various aspects of life. Resilience refers to the ability to bounce back from setbacks, adapt to change, and overcome challenges. In social situations, resilience plays a key role in effectively managing interpersonal relationships, navigating conflicts, and maintaining a positive outlook despite adversity. Developing resilience in social settings requires a combination of self-awareness, emotional intelligence, and effective communication skills.

One of the first steps in building resilience in social situations is cultivating self-awareness. This involves understanding one's strengths, weaknesses, values, and beliefs. By developing a clear sense of self, individuals can better navigate social interactions and respond to challenges in a way that aligns with their authentic self. Self-awareness also allows individuals to recognize their triggers and emotional responses in social situations, enabling them to regulate their emotions and make more informed decisions.

In addition to self-awareness, emotional intelligence is an essential component of resilience in social situations. Emotional intelligence encompasses the ability to recognize, understand, and manage one's own emotions as well as the emotions of others. By being aware of one's emotions and the impact they have on others, individuals can better navigate social interactions, resolve conflicts, and build strong relationships. Developing emotional intelligence involves practicing empathy, active listening, and effective communication skills, all of which are essential for building resilience in social settings.

Effective communication is another key aspect of building resilience in social situations. Clear and open communication is essential for expressing one's thoughts, feelings, and needs, as well as for resolving conflicts and building trust in relationships. By honing their communication skills, individuals can effectively convey their ideas, assert boundaries, and seek support when needed. Effective communication also involves active listening and being able to empathize with others, which fosters understanding and connection in social interactions.

Building resilience in social situations also requires the ability to set boundaries and assert oneself effectively. Boundaries are essential for maintaining a healthy balance in relationships and safeguarding one's well-being. By setting clear boundaries and asserting oneself assertively yet respectfully, individuals can protect themselves from harmful or disrespectful behavior, communicate their needs and preferences, and build stronger and more fulfilling relationships. Assertiveness involves expressing oneself confidently and standing up for one's rights and beliefs without being aggressive or passive.

Lastly, developing resilience in social situations involves cultivating a positive mindset and adopting healthy coping strategies. Maintaining a positive outlook can help individuals navigate challenges and setbacks more effectively, as well as build resilience in the face of adversity. By focusing on strengths, practicing gratitude, and reframing negative thoughts, individuals can build resilience and maintain a sense of optimism in social situations. Additionally, developing healthy coping strategies, such as self-care, mindfulness, and seeking support from others, can help individuals manage stress, anxiety, and other negative emotions that may arise in social situations. By developing these skills and strategies, individuals can navigate social interactions with confidence, adaptability, and grace, ultimately leading to stronger relationships, increased well-being, and greater success in various aspects of life. Building resilience in social situations is not only beneficial for individuals but also for society as a whole, as it fosters understanding, respect, and empathy in interpersonal relationships. By prioritizing resilience in social settings, individuals can cultivate a more inclusive, supportive, and harmonious society.

Chapter 11: Teamwork and Collaboration

- DEVELOPING TEAMWORK skills and cooperation with others

Developing teamwork skills and cooperation with others are crucial elements in achieving success in any professional or academic setting. Effective teamwork involves working collaboratively with others to achieve common goals, share ideas and resources, and communicate effectively. Cooperation with others requires a willingness to listen to different perspectives, compromise when necessary, and contribute to the overall success of the team. In this article, we will explore the importance of teamwork skills and cooperation with others, as well as practical strategies for developing these essential skills.

One of the key benefits of developing teamwork skills is the ability to leverage the collective talents and strengths of a group. When individuals work together towards a common goal, they can achieve outcomes that would be difficult or impossible to accomplish on their own. By fostering a collaborative environment where team members can share their unique skills and expertise, organizations can tap into a diverse range of perspectives and ideas. This diversity of thought can lead to innovative solutions, improved decision-making, and enhanced problem-solving capabilities.

Moreover, effective teamwork can also enhance employee morale and job satisfaction. When individuals feel supported and valued by their team members, they are more likely to be engaged and motivated to perform at their best. Working as part of a cohesive team can also create a sense of camaraderie and belonging, fostering positive relationships and reducing stress in the workplace.

By fostering a positive team dynamic, organizations can create a more positive and collaborative working environment, leading to increased productivity and job satisfaction.

In addition to the benefits for individuals, developing teamwork skills can also have a positive impact on organizational performance. Teams that work well together are often more efficient and productive, as they can leverage each other's strengths and work towards common goals. Effective teamwork can also improve communication and coordination within an organization, leading to better alignment of objectives and more streamlined processes. By fostering a culture of teamwork and collaboration, organizations can create a more cohesive and resilient workforce, capable of adapting to changing circumstances and driving continuous improvement.

Cooperation with others is also essential for success in academic settings. Whether working on group projects, conducting research, or participating in extracurricular activities, students often need to collaborate with their peers to achieve their academic goals. Cooperation requires effective communication, active listening, and a willingness to work together towards a shared objective. By developing cooperation skills, students can enhance their ability to work effectively with others, navigate conflicts, and contribute positively to group dynamics.

To develop teamwork skills and cooperation with others, individuals can take a number of practical steps. One of the first steps is to build strong relationships with team members based on trust, respect, and open communication. By establishing a foundation of mutual respect and understanding, team members can create a positive and supportive working environment that enables effective collaboration. Encouraging open and honest communication, actively listening to others, and providing constructive feedback can help to build trust and strengthen relationships within the team.

Another important aspect of developing teamwork skills is understanding and valuing the diverse perspectives and experiences of team members. Recognizing and appreciating the unique skills and talents that each individual brings to the team can help to foster a culture of inclusivity and respect. By embracing diversity and promoting a culture of inclusion, teams can leverage the strengths and abilities of all team members, leading to improved collaboration and better outcomes.

Effective teamwork also requires clear goals, roles, and responsibilities for each team member. By establishing clear expectations and accountability within the team, individuals can work together more efficiently and effectively towards common objectives. Setting SMART goals (specific, measurable, achievable, relevant, and time-bound), defining roles and responsibilities, and creating a plan for achieving objectives can help to keep team members focused and aligned towards a shared vision.

Another key component of developing teamwork skills is effective communication. Clear and open communication is essential for successful collaboration, as it enables team members to share ideas, provide feedback, and coordinate their efforts towards achieving common goals. By promoting a culture of transparency, active listening, and effective communication, individuals can enhance their ability to work together, resolve conflicts, and make informed decisions as a team. By fostering a culture of collaboration, communication, and inclusivity, individuals can enhance their ability to work effectively with others, leverage the strengths and abilities of team members, and achieve common objectives. By valuing diverse perspectives, setting clear goals and roles, and promoting open communication, organizations and teams can create a positive and supportive working environment that fosters innovation, productivity, and success. By investing in the development of teamwork skills and cooperation with others, individuals can enhance their personal and professional growth, build strong relationships, and achieve collective success.

- Working together towards common goals and projects

In today's fast-paced and interconnected world, collaboration and teamwork are more important than ever. Working together towards common goals and projects can lead to greater success and innovation. When individuals come together, combining their unique skills, perspectives, and expertise, they can achieve more than they ever could on their own.

One of the key benefits of working together towards common goals and projects is the ability to leverage the diverse strengths and talents of team members. Each person brings their own unique set of skills and experiences to the table, and by working together, they can complement each other's strengths and fill in each other's weaknesses. This diversity of perspectives and abilities allows the team to come up with creative solutions and approaches that may not have been possible if each individual had been working in isolation.

Furthermore, collaboration fosters a sense of camaraderie and mutual support among team members. When individuals work together towards a common goal, they develop a sense of shared purpose and commitment that can help them overcome challenges and obstacles. This sense of unity can create a positive work environment and foster a culture of trust and respect among team members.

In addition, working together towards common goals and projects can lead to increased efficiency and productivity. By pooling resources and dividing tasks among team members, projects can be completed more quickly and with higher quality. This is particularly true in complex projects that require a variety of skills and expertise. When individuals work together, they can focus on their areas of strength and specialization, while trusting their teammates to handle other aspects of the project.

Collaboration also promotes learning and personal growth. When individuals work together towards common goals and projects, they have the opportunity to learn from each other and expand their knowledge and skills. By working with others who have different perspectives and experiences, individuals can broaden their understanding of a subject and develop new ways of thinking and problem-solving. This can lead to personal growth and development, as well as increased creativity and innovation.

In closing, collaboration can lead to greater success and achievement. By working together towards common goals and projects, individuals can achieve outcomes that are greater than the sum of their parts. When individuals combine their efforts and resources, they can accomplish things that would have been impossible for them to achieve alone. This can lead to greater success, recognition, and satisfaction for all team members. By collaborating with others, individuals can leverage their diverse strengths, foster a sense of camaraderie and support, increase efficiency and productivity, promote learning and personal growth, and achieve greater success and achievement. By coming together and combining their unique skills and perspectives, individuals can create innovative solutions and make a positive impact on the world around them.

Chapter 12: Public Speaking and Presentation Skills

- TIPS FOR IMPROVING public speaking and presenting abilities

Public speaking and presenting are skills that are essential for success in both professional and academic settings. Whether you are giving a presentation at work, speaking at a conference, or delivering a speech in front of a classroom, being able to effectively communicate your ideas is crucial. However, for many people, the thought of speaking in front of a group can be intimidating and nerve-wracking. Fortunately, there are strategies and tips that can help improve your public speaking and presenting abilities.

One of the keys to successful public speaking is preparation. It is important to thoroughly prepare for your presentation by researching your topic, organizing your thoughts, and creating a clear and concise outline. This will help you feel more confident and prepared when it comes time to speak. Additionally, practicing your presentation multiple times can help you become more comfortable with the material and improve your delivery. This can also help you identify any areas that may need additional clarification or explanation.

Another important aspect of public speaking is understanding your audience. Before giving a presentation, take the time to consider who will be in the audience and tailor your message accordingly. This might mean adjusting your language, tone, or examples to better resonate with your listeners. Additionally, engaging with your audience by asking questions, encouraging participation, and making eye contact can help create a more interactive and engaging experience for everyone involved.

Nonverbal communication plays a significant role in public speaking as well. Pay attention to your body language, facial expressions, and gestures while speaking. Maintaining good posture, making eye contact, and using hand gestures can help convey confidence and credibility to your audience. Additionally, be mindful of your tone of voice and speaking pace, as these can also impact how your message is received.

Furthermore, incorporating visuals into your presentation can enhance the effectiveness of your message. Visual aids such as PowerPoint slides, graphs, charts, or videos can help illustrate key points, break up content, and keep your audience engaged. However, it is important to use visuals sparingly and strategically, as too many distractions can take away from your message. Make sure your visuals are clear, relevant, and easy to read from a distance.

Another tip for improving public speaking and presenting abilities is to practice active listening. This involves actively engaging with your audience by paying attention to their reactions, responding to questions or feedback, and adjusting your presentation as needed. By listening to your audience, you can better understand their needs and interests, which can help you tailor your message to be more engaging and relevant.

Lastly, remember that public speaking is a skill that can be developed and improved over time. It is normal to feel nervous or anxious before speaking in front of a group, but with practice and perseverance, you can become a more confident and effective speaker. By following these tips and strategies, you can enhance your public speaking and presenting abilities and become a more persuasive and influential communicator in both professional and academic settings.

- Overcoming stage fright and speaking in front of a group

Public speaking is a common fear shared by many individuals, known as glossophobia. It is a fear of speaking in front of an audience, whether it be a small group or a large crowd. The fear of public speaking can often result in physical symptoms such as a racing heart, sweating, trembling, and even stuttering. This fear can be debilitating and can prevent individuals from fully showcasing their knowledge and expertise. However, it is possible to overcome stage fright and improve your public speaking skills with practice, preparation, and a positive mindset.

One of the first steps in overcoming stage fright is to understand the root cause of your fear. The fear of public speaking is often attributed to a fear of judgment or failure. Individuals may worry about making mistakes, forgetting their lines, or being perceived negatively by the audience. By identifying the specific triggers of your fear, you can begin to address them and develop strategies to minimize their impact. Additionally, recognizing that nervousness is a natural response to the unfamiliar situation of public speaking can help alleviate some of the anxiety associated with it.

Preparation is key when it comes to overcoming stage fright. The more prepared you are, the more confident you will feel when delivering your speech. Take the time to research your topic thoroughly, organize your thoughts, and create a structured outline for your presentation. Practice your speech multiple times, either in front of a mirror or with a trusted friend or family member. Rehearsing your speech will help you become more comfortable with the material and reduce the likelihood of mistakes during the actual presentation. Additionally, familiarizing yourself with the venue and equipment, such as microphones and projectors, can help you feel more at ease on the day of your presentation.

Another tip for overcoming stage fright is to focus on your audience and their needs. Remember that your presentation is not about you, but rather about sharing valuable information or insights with your audience. By shifting your focus away from yourself and towards your audience, you can reduce feelings of self-consciousness and anxiety. Practice active listening and engage with your audience by asking questions, encouraging participation, and incorporating anecdotes or examples that resonate with them. Building a connection with your audience can help create a more relaxed and engaging atmosphere during your presentation.

Visual aids can also be a helpful tool in overcoming stage fright. Utilizing visual aids such as PowerPoint slides, videos, or handouts can help reinforce your message and keep your audience engaged. Visual aids can serve as a visual cue for you to stay on track and can provide a mental break for both you and your audience. However, it is important to use visual aids sparingly and make sure they enhance your presentation rather than detract from it. Practice using your visual aids before the presentation to ensure they are working properly and do not cause any distractions.

In addition to preparation and practice, adopting a positive mindset can greatly impact your ability to overcome stage fright. Instead of focusing on potential mistakes or negative outcomes, try to envision a successful and engaging presentation. Visualize yourself speaking confidently and effectively, and imagine yourself receiving positive feedback from your audience. Positive self-talk can also be beneficial in boosting your confidence and reducing anxiety. Remind yourself of your expertise, experience, and preparation, and trust in your ability to deliver a compelling presentation. Remember that mistakes are a natural part of public speaking and can even make your presentation more authentic and relatable to your audience.

Lastly, seeking feedback and support from others can be invaluable in overcoming stage fright. Ask for constructive feedback from trusted colleagues, friends, or mentors on your presentation style, delivery, and content. Constructive feedback can help you identify areas for improvement and provide you with valuable insights on how to enhance your public speaking skills. Additionally, consider joining a public speaking group or taking a public speaking course to practice your skills in a supportive environment. Surrounding yourself with like-minded individuals who share a similar goal of improving their public speaking skills can help boost your confidence and motivation. By understanding the root cause of your fear, preparing thoroughly, focusing on your audience, utilizing visual aids, maintaining a positive mindset, and seeking feedback and support, you can gradually overcome your stage fright and become a more confident and effective public speaker. Remember that public speaking is a skill that can be developed and refined over time, and with persistence and determination, you can conquer your fear and deliver impactful presentations with ease.

Chapter 13: Problem-Solving Skills

- TEACHING CHILDREN problem-solving strategies

Teaching children problem-solving strategies is crucial for their cognitive development and future success. Problem-solving skills are essential in daily life and can be applied to a wide range of situations, from solving math problems to resolving conflicts with friends. By teaching children effective problem-solving strategies, we can empower them to tackle challenges with confidence and resilience.

One key strategy for teaching children problem-solving skills is to encourage them to break down problems into smaller, more manageable parts. This approach helps children see the big picture and identify specific steps they can take to solve the problem. For example, when faced with a challenging math problem, children can start by identifying the key information and breaking the problem down into smaller steps. By breaking the problem down into manageable parts, children can approach problem-solving in a systematic and structured way.

Another important strategy for teaching children problem-solving skills is to encourage them to think creatively and outside the box. Creative thinking helps children come up with innovative solutions to complex problems and allows them to explore different perspectives. For example, when faced with a creative writing assignment, children can think outside the box by brainstorming unique ideas and approaches. By encouraging children to think creatively, we can help them develop their problem-solving skills and foster a sense of curiosity and exploration.

Furthermore, teaching children problem-solving strategies involves guiding them through the process of trial and error. When children encounter obstacles or setbacks while trying to solve a problem, it is important to encourage them to persevere and learn from their mistakes. By teaching children that it is okay to make mistakes and that they can learn from them, we can help them develop resilience and perseverance in the face of challenges. For example, when children are struggling with a difficult puzzle, they can try different approaches and learn from their mistakes to eventually find a solution.

In addition, collaborative problem-solving is an effective strategy for teaching children problem-solving skills. By encouraging children to work together in groups or pairs, they can learn from each other's perspectives and ideas. Collaboration helps children develop their communication and teamwork skills, which are essential for solving complex problems. For example, when working on a group project, children can learn to listen to each other's ideas, communicate effectively, and compromise to reach a consensus. By encouraging collaboration, we can help children develop their problem-solving skills in a supportive and cooperative environment.

Moreover, teaching children problem-solving strategies can also involve providing them with opportunities to practice their skills in real-world situations. By giving children hands-on experiences and challenges, we can help them apply their problem-solving skills in practical ways. For example, children can participate in science experiments, engineering projects, or mock scenarios that require them to think critically and come up with solutions. By allowing children to practice problem-solving in real-world contexts, we can help them build confidence and competence in their abilities. By encouraging children to break down problems, think creatively, learn from mistakes, collaborate with others, and practice their skills in real-world situations, we can help them become confident and effective problem solvers. By fostering a supportive and engaging learning environment, we can empower children to approach challenges with curiosity, resilience, and innovation. Through effective problem-solving strategies, we can equip children with the skills they need to navigate the complexities of the world around them and achieve their full potential.

- Encouraging creative thinking and decision-making

Encouraging creative thinking and decision-making is essential in today's rapidly changing and highly competitive business environment. Creative thinking allows individuals to generate innovative ideas and solutions, while effective decision-making ensures that those ideas are implemented in a timely and efficient manner. By fostering a culture of creativity and encouraging employees to think outside the box, organizations can stay ahead of the curve and drive long-term success.

One way to encourage creative thinking and decision-making is to create a supportive and inclusive work environment where employees feel empowered to share their ideas and opinions. When employees feel valued and respected, they are more likely to take risks and think creatively. This can be achieved through open communication, regular feedback, and opportunities for collaboration. By fostering a culture of trust and respect, organizations can create a safe space for employees to explore new ideas and approaches.

In addition to creating a supportive work environment, organizations can also promote creative thinking and decision-making by providing employees with the tools and resources they need to succeed. This may include access to training and development opportunities, as well as technology and equipment that support innovation. By investing in their employees and giving them the tools they need to succeed, organizations can empower them to think creatively and make informed decisions.

Another way to encourage creative thinking and decision-making is to reward and recognize employees for their contributions. By celebrating successes and highlighting innovative ideas, organizations can inspire employees to continue thinking creatively and making bold decisions. This can be done through formal recognition programs, as well as more informal gestures such as praise and thank you notes. By showing employees that their efforts are valued and appreciated, organizations can motivate them to continue pushing the boundaries of what is possible.

In short, organizations can encourage creative thinking and decision-making by creating a culture of experimentation and learning. By encouraging employees to try new things and learn from their mistakes, organizations can foster a culture of continuous improvement and innovation. This can be achieved through regular brainstorming sessions, workshops, and other opportunities for employees to collaborate and share ideas. By creating a culture of experimentation and learning, organizations can lay the foundation for long-term success and sustainable growth. By creating a supportive and inclusive work environment, providing employees with the tools and resources they need to succeed, rewarding and recognizing their efforts, and fostering a culture of experimentation and learning, organizations can empower their employees to think creatively and make bold decisions. By taking these steps, organizations can drive innovation, improve performance, and position themselves for long-term success.

Chapter 14: Time Management and Organization

- LEARNING TO MANAGE time effectively and stay organized

Time management and organization are two essential skills that play a pivotal role in achieving success in both personal and professional endeavors. Learning to manage time effectively involves a combination of self-discipline, efficient planning, and prioritization of tasks. By mastering these skills, individuals can maximize productivity, reduce stress, and achieve their goals in a more efficient manner. In this article, we will explore various strategies and techniques that can help individuals learn how to manage their time effectively and stay organized.

One of the first steps in learning to manage time effectively is to establish clear goals and objectives. By setting specific, measurable, achievable, relevant, and time-bound (SMART) goals, individuals can create a roadmap for their tasks and projects. This allows them to prioritize their activities based on importance and deadlines, ensuring that they allocate their time and resources effectively. Additionally, setting goals helps individuals stay focused and motivated, as they have a clear vision of what they want to achieve and the steps needed to get there.

Another important aspect of time management is creating a daily or weekly schedule. By organizing tasks and activities into a structured timetable, individuals can allocate time for each task, ensuring that they make progress towards their goals. Scheduling tasks based on their priority and deadlines helps individuals avoid procrastination and stay on track with their work. Moreover, having a schedule allows individuals to identify potential conflicts or bottlenecks in their workload, enabling them to make adjustments as needed to ensure that they meet their deadlines.

In addition to setting goals and creating a schedule, individuals can also benefit from using time management tools and techniques to optimize their productivity. For example, using a calendar or planner to track deadlines, appointments, and tasks can help individuals stay organized and ensure that they do not miss important deadlines or commitments. Similarly, using to-do lists or task management apps can help individuals break down their work into smaller, more manageable chunks, making it easier to prioritize and complete tasks efficiently.

Furthermore, individuals can also benefit from practicing time management techniques such as the Pomodoro Technique or time blocking. The Pomodoro Technique involves breaking work into intervals of focused work (typically 25 minutes) followed by a short break, helping individuals maintain focus and avoid burnout. Time blocking involves setting aside specific blocks of time for different tasks or activities, allowing individuals to dedicate their full attention to each task without distractions. By incorporating these techniques into their daily routine, individuals can improve their focus, efficiency, and productivity.

It is also important for individuals to learn how to effectively delegate tasks and responsibilities to others. Delegation allows individuals to focus on high-priority tasks while entrusting less critical tasks to others who may be better suited to handle them. By delegating tasks, individuals can free up their time and energy to focus on more important activities, helping them achieve their goals more efficiently. Additionally, delegation helps individuals build trust and collaboration with others, fostering a more productive and effective work environment. By setting clear goals, creating a schedule, using time management tools and techniques, practicing delegation, individuals can improve their efficiency, reduce stress, and achieve success in their personal and professional lives. By incorporating these strategies into their daily routine, individuals can gain greater control over their time and workload, allowing them to achieve their goals more effectively.

- Balancing social activities with school and other responsibilities

Balancing social activities with school and other responsibilities is a common challenge that many individuals face, especially in today's fast-paced and demanding world. It can be difficult to find the right balance between socializing with friends, participating in extracurricular activities, and meeting academic obligations. However, with some careful planning and time management strategies, it is possible to strike a healthy balance that allows for both social engagement and academic success.

One key to balancing social activities with school and other responsibilities is to prioritize and set clear boundaries. It is important to identify your most important commitments, such as studying for exams, completing assignments, and attending classes, and make sure to allocate time for these activities first. Once these priorities are established, you can then schedule social activities and other commitments around them. Creating a weekly or monthly calendar can be a helpful tool for visualizing how your time is being spent and ensuring that you are dedicating enough time to each area of your life.

Another important aspect of balancing social activities with school and other responsibilities is to learn to say no when necessary. It can be tempting to say yes to every social invitation or opportunity that comes your way, but it is important to recognize your limits and prioritize your own well-being. If you are feeling overwhelmed or stressed, it is okay to decline an invitation or take a break from socializing in order to focus on your schoolwork or other responsibilities. Setting boundaries and being honest with yourself and others about your availability and limitations can help prevent burnout and ensure that you are able to maintain a healthy balance in your life.

Additionally, finding ways to combine social activities with academic responsibilities can help make balancing these aspects of your life more manageable. For example, studying with friends or participating in study groups can allow you to socialize while also staying on top of your schoolwork. Similarly, joining clubs or organizations related to your academic interests can provide opportunities for socializing and networking while also enhancing your academic experience. By finding ways to integrate social activities into your academic routine, you can make the most of your time and create a more fulfilling and balanced lifestyle.

It is also important to practice self-care and prioritize your mental and physical health when balancing social activities with school and other responsibilities. Taking time for yourself to relax, exercise, and engage in activities that bring you joy can help reduce stress and prevent burnout. Making sure to get enough sleep, eat well, and engage in regular physical activity can also help improve your overall well-being and energy levels, making it easier to juggle the demands of school and social activities. Remember that taking care of yourself is essential for maintaining a healthy balance in your life and ensuring that you are able to perform at your best in all areas. By prioritizing and setting boundaries, learning to say no when necessary, finding ways to integrate social activities with academic responsibilities, and practicing self-care, you can create a fulfilling and balanced lifestyle that supports your overall well-being and success. Remember that it is okay to ask for help or seek support when needed, and that finding the right balance may require some trial and error. With determination, patience, and a positive attitude, you can navigate the challenges of balancing social activities with school and other responsibilities and achieve your goals.

Chapter 15: Goal Setting and Achievement

- SETTING ACHIEVABLE goals and working towards them

Setting achievable goals is an essential aspect of personal growth and success. Goals provide direction and motivation, helping individuals to focus their energy and efforts on specific outcomes. However, it is important to set goals that are realistic and attainable, as setting overly ambitious or unattainable goals can lead to frustration and disappointment. By setting achievable goals, individuals can build confidence, track their progress, and ultimately reach their full potential.

One key aspect of setting achievable goals is ensuring they are specific and measurable. Vague or general goals can be difficult to track progress towards, making it challenging to determine whether they have been achieved. By setting specific and measurable goals, individuals can clearly define what they want to accomplish and establish concrete criteria for success. For example, instead of setting a goal to "exercise more," a more specific and measurable goal could be to "run three times a week for 30 minutes each time. " This allows individuals to track their progress and adjust their efforts as needed to achieve their goal.

In addition to being specific and measurable, achievable goals should also be challenging yet realistic. Setting goals that are too easy may not provide enough motivation, while setting goals that are too difficult can be discouraging. By setting goals that are challenging but attainable, individuals can push themselves to strive for excellence while also setting themselves up for success. It is important to consider one's abilities, resources, and circumstances when setting goals to ensure they are within reach. For example, setting a goal to run a marathon within a few weeks may not be realistic for someone who is just starting a fitness routine, but setting a goal to run a 5k in a few months may be more achievable.

Another important aspect of setting achievable goals is breaking them down into smaller, manageable steps. Large or long-term goals can feel overwhelming and daunting, making it difficult to stay motivated and focused. By breaking goals down into smaller tasks or milestones, individuals can make progress gradually and build momentum towards their ultimate goal. This approach can help individuals stay on track, celebrate small victories along the way, and stay motivated to continue working towards their goal. For example, if the ultimate goal is to write a book, breaking it down into smaller tasks such as outlining ones, researching topics, and writing a certain number of pages each day can make the goal more achievable.

Furthermore, setting achievable goals requires commitment, persistence, and resilience. Achieving goals takes time, effort, and dedication, and setbacks or obstacles are inevitable along the way. It is important for individuals to stay focused on their goals, remain flexible in their approach, and persevere through challenges to ultimately achieve success. By maintaining a positive attitude, staying motivated, and learning from failures, individuals can overcome obstacles and continue working towards their goals. It is also helpful to seek support from friends, family, or mentors to provide encouragement, accountability, and guidance as individuals work towards their goals. By setting specific, measurable, challenging yet realistic goals, breaking them down into smaller steps, and committing to their achievement, individuals can make progress, build confidence, and ultimately reach their full potential. Setting achievable goals provides direction, motivation, and a sense of purpose, helping individuals to focus their energy and efforts on specific outcomes. By following these guidelines and strategies for setting achievable goals, individuals can set themselves up for success and work towards achieving their dreams and aspirations.

- Celebrating successes and learning from setbacks

Celebrating successes and learning from setbacks are essential components of personal and professional growth. Both experiences offer valuable lessons and insights that can help individuals and organizations improve and achieve their goals. It is important to acknowledge and celebrate successes to boost morale, foster a positive work culture, and motivate individuals to continue striving for excellence. On the other hand, setbacks provide opportunities for reflection, learning, and resilience-building. By understanding the reasons behind setbacks and implementing strategies to overcome challenges, individuals can emerge stronger and more prepared for future obstacles.

First and foremost, celebrating successes is crucial for recognizing and rewarding achievements. It is important to acknowledge the hard work and dedication that individuals put into their work, as well as the positive outcomes that result from their efforts. By celebrating successes, individuals are more likely to feel valued, appreciated, and motivated to continue performing at a high level. This can help boost morale, increase job satisfaction, and create a positive work environment where individuals feel recognized and supported.

Furthermore, celebrating successes can also help foster a culture of recognition and appreciation within an organization. When successes are celebrated, it sends a clear message that hard work and excellence are valued and rewarded. This can motivate individuals to strive for greatness and take pride in their achievements. In addition, celebrating successes can also help build team unity and collaboration, as it encourages individuals to support and celebrate each other's accomplishments. This can help create a positive and supportive work culture where individuals feel connected and motivated to work together towards common goals.

In addition to celebrating successes, it is also important to learn from setbacks and failures. Setbacks are inevitable in any personal or professional journey, but how individuals respond to these challenges can greatly impact their growth and development. Instead of viewing setbacks as failures, it is essential to see them as opportunities for learning, growth, and improvement. By reflecting on setbacks and identifying the reasons behind them, individuals can gain valuable insights into what went wrong and how they can avoid similar mistakes in the future.

Moreover, learning from setbacks can also help individuals build resilience and develop problem-solving skills. Dealing with setbacks requires individuals to adapt, think creatively, and stay persistent in the face of challenges. By overcoming setbacks, individuals can build confidence in their ability to navigate obstacles and emerge stronger and more resilient. This can help individuals develop a growth mindset, where setbacks are viewed as learning opportunities rather than insurmountable obstacles.

Furthermore, learning from setbacks can also lead to innovation and improvement. By recognizing mistakes and areas for improvement, individuals can implement strategies to prevent similar setbacks in the future. This can lead to continuous improvement, innovation, and growth within an organization. By embracing setbacks as learning opportunities, individuals can create a culture of continuous learning, adaptation, and improvement that can drive success and achievement in the long run. By acknowledging and celebrating successes, individuals can boost morale, foster a positive work culture, and motivate individuals to continue striving for excellence. On the other hand, setbacks provide valuable opportunities for reflection, learning, and resilience-building. By understanding the reasons behind setbacks and implementing strategies to overcome challenges, individuals can emerge stronger and more prepared for future obstacles. By embracing both successes and setbacks with a growth mindset, individuals can create a culture of continuous learning, improvement, and innovation that can drive success and achievement in the long run.

Chapter 16; Developing Leadership Skills

- ENCOURAGING LEADERSHIP qualities in children

Leadership qualities are essential for success in both personal and professional endeavors. While some individuals may possess natural leadership abilities, it is important to cultivate and encourage these traits in children from a young age. By instilling a sense of confidence, communication skills, and empathy in children, we can help them develop into effective leaders who are able to inspire and motivate others.

One of the key ways to encourage leadership qualities in children is to provide them with opportunities to take on leadership roles and responsibilities. This can be done in a variety of settings, such as school, sports teams, or community organizations. By giving children the chance to lead a project, organize an event, or mentor their peers, they can develop important skills like decision-making, problem-solving, and teamwork. These experiences not only help children build their leadership abilities, but also boost their self-confidence and sense of accomplishment.

Another important aspect of fostering leadership qualities in children is to teach them effective communication skills. Leaders must be able to clearly articulate their ideas, listen actively to others, and adapt their communication style to different situations and audiences. By encouraging children to practice public speaking, engage in group discussions, and collaborate with their peers, we can help them become more effective communicators. Additionally, teaching children how to actively listen, show empathy, and resolve conflicts peacefully can help them build stronger relationships and connect with others in a meaningful way.

Empathy is another crucial trait that leaders must possess, as it allows them to understand and connect with the emotions and perspectives of others. By teaching children to be empathetic towards their peers, family members, and community members, we can help them develop a strong sense of compassion and understanding. Empathy enables children to build stronger relationships, resolve conflicts peacefully, and collaborate effectively with others. By encouraging children to consider the feelings and needs of others, we can help them become more caring and socially responsible individuals.

In addition to providing children with opportunities to lead, teaching them effective communication skills, and fostering empathy, it is important to model leadership behavior for children to emulate. As adults, parents, teachers, and mentors play a crucial role in shaping the leadership development of children. By demonstrating positive leadership qualities such as integrity, accountability, and resilience, adults can serve as role models for children to look up to. By showing children how to lead by example, take responsibility for their actions, and persevere in the face of challenges, adults can instill important values and behaviors that will guide children in their own leadership journeys.

- Inspiring confidence and responsibility in a group setting

Inspiring confidence and responsibility within a group setting is essential for fostering a positive and productive team dynamic. When individuals feel empowered and capable within a group, they are more likely to take ownership of their actions and contribute to the overall success of the team. Building confidence and responsibility involves creating a supportive and inclusive environment where team members feel valued, respected, and motivated to do their best work.

One way to inspire confidence and responsibility within a group setting is to provide clear expectations and goals for the team. When everyone knows what is expected of them and what the team is working towards, they are more likely to take responsibility for their role in achieving those goals. Setting specific objectives and milestones can help to keep the team focused and motivated, while also providing a framework for evaluating progress and performance.

Another important aspect of inspiring confidence and responsibility in a group setting is to provide opportunities for individual growth and development. Encouraging team members to take on new challenges, learn new skills, and expand their knowledge can help to boost their confidence and sense of self-efficacy. By fostering a culture of continuous learning and development, team members can develop the skills and knowledge they need to take responsibility for their work and contribute effectively to the team.

In addition to setting clear expectations and providing development opportunities, it is also important to create a supportive and inclusive team culture that values diversity and collaboration. When team members feel supported by their colleagues and leaders, they are more likely to feel confident in their abilities and take responsibility for their actions. Building strong relationships within the team and promoting open communication can help to create a sense of trust and mutual respect, which can in turn foster confidence and responsibility among team members.

To culminate, it is important for leaders to lead by example when it comes to inspiring confidence and responsibility within a group setting. Demonstrating confidence in one's own abilities, taking responsibility for one's actions, and showing a willingness to learn and grow can help to inspire others to do the same. By modeling the behavior and attitudes that are expected from team members, leaders can create a positive and empowering environment where confidence and responsibility thrive. By setting clear expectations, providing opportunities for growth and development, fostering a supportive and inclusive team culture, and leading by example, leaders can create an environment where team members feel empowered and motivated to do their best work. By instilling a sense of confidence and responsibility in each team member, teams can work together more effectively, achieve their goals, and overcome challenges with resilience and determination.

Chapter 17: Networking and Building Connections

- UNDERSTANDING THE importance of networking and building connections

Networking and building connections are essential components of a successful professional career. In today's interconnected world, the ability to establish and maintain relationships with others can open up numerous opportunities for growth and advancement. Whether you are just starting out in your career or are a seasoned professional, networking can help you expand your knowledge, gain access to new resources, and increase your visibility in your field.

One of the key benefits of networking is the opportunity to exchange ideas and information with others. By connecting with individuals who have different perspectives and experiences, you can gain valuable insights that can help you solve problems, generate new ideas, and improve your skills. Networking can also provide you with access to new resources, such as job leads, industry contacts, and professional development opportunities. By building relationships with others in your field, you can stay informed about the latest trends and developments, which can help you stay competitive in your industry.

In addition to providing access to new resources and information, networking can also help you increase your visibility and credibility in your field. When you establish relationships with other professionals, you create a network of individuals who can vouch for your skills and abilities. By building a reputation as a reliable and knowledgeable professional, you can attract new opportunities and collaborations. Networking can also help you establish yourself as a thought leader in your field, as you share your expertise with others and contribute to the ongoing conversation in your industry.

Networking can also have a significant impact on your career advancement. In many industries, the majority of job opportunities are never advertised publicly, but are instead filled through word-of-mouth referrals and recommendations. By building strong relationships with other professionals, you increase your chances of being recommended for new opportunities. Networking can also help you build a support system of mentors, colleagues, and friends who can provide guidance, advice, and encouragement as you navigate your career path. By nurturing these relationships, you can create a strong foundation of support that can help you achieve your goals and overcome obstacles.

While networking is important for professionals in all industries, it is especially critical for those in fields that are rapidly evolving or highly competitive. In these industries, staying connected with others is essential for staying informed about the latest developments, accessing new opportunities, and building a strong professional reputation. By actively participating in networking events, conferences, and online communities, you can expand your network and stay ahead of the curve in your field. Networking can also help you build relationships with influential individuals who can provide valuable advice, introductions, and opportunities for collaboration. By actively engaging with others, sharing your expertise, and building relationships with individuals who can support and mentor you, you can create a strong network of connections that can help you achieve your goals and navigate the challenges of your career. Whether you are just starting out or are a seasoned professional, investing time and effort into networking can pay off in countless ways, from opening up new opportunities to helping you stay competitive and relevant in your industry.

- **Cultivating relationships for future opportunities**

Building and maintaining relationships is a crucial aspect of professional success. Cultivating relationships with colleagues, mentors, clients, and industry contacts can open doors to valuable opportunities in the future. By investing time and effort into fostering these relationships, individuals can build a network of contacts that can provide support, guidance, and potential leads for career advancement.

One of the key benefits of cultivating relationships for future opportunities is the potential for mentorship and guidance. Building strong relationships with experienced professionals in your field can provide valuable insights and advice that can help you navigate your career path. Mentors can offer valuable feedback, share their own experiences, and provide guidance on how to overcome challenges and achieve your goals. By investing in these relationships, individuals can gain access to valuable resources and support that can help them succeed in their careers.

In addition to mentorship, cultivating relationships can also open doors to potential job opportunities. Networking with industry contacts and staying connected with former colleagues can create a pipeline of potential leads for future job opportunities. By building and maintaining relationships with a wide range of professionals in your field, you increase the likelihood of learning about job openings before they are widely advertised. Additionally, having a strong network of contacts can make it easier to get recommendations and referrals for potential job opportunities, increasing your chances of landing a desirable position.

Furthermore, cultivating relationships can also lead to opportunities for collaboration and partnerships. Building strong relationships with individuals in your industry can lead to potential collaborations on projects, partnerships on ventures, or opportunities to work together on shared goals. By investing in these relationships and fostering open communication and trust, individuals can create opportunities for mutual benefit and growth. Collaborating with others in your industry can help you expand your skills, knowledge, and network, while also potentially leading to new and exciting opportunities for career advancement.

In order to effectively cultivate relationships for future opportunities, it is important to be proactive in building and maintaining connections with others. This means taking the initiative to reach out to new contacts, attending networking events, and staying in touch with existing connections. Building relationships takes time and effort, so it is important to invest in these connections consistently over time. This may involve setting aside time each week to reach out to contacts, schedule meetings or coffee chats, or attend industry events where you can meet new people and expand your network.

Another key aspect of cultivating relationships for future opportunities is the importance of building trust and credibility with others. Trust is a crucial element of any successful relationship, and it is important to be honest, reliable, and respectful in all of your interactions with others. Building trust with your colleagues, mentors, and industry contacts can help you establish strong and lasting relationships that can provide support and opportunities in the future. By demonstrating your reliability, integrity, and professionalism, you can build a positive reputation and earn the trust of others in your network.

In addition, it is important to be strategic in your approach to cultivating relationships for future opportunities. This means identifying key individuals within your network who have the potential to influence your career path and focusing on building stronger connections with them. By targeting specific individuals who can provide valuable insights, mentorship, or opportunities for advancement, you can maximize the impact of your networking efforts. It is also important to be clear about your goals and objectives in cultivating relationships, so that you can focus on building connections that align with your long-term career aspirations. By investing time and effort into building and maintaining relationships with colleagues, mentors, clients, and industry contacts, individuals can create a network of support and opportunities that can help them achieve their career goals. Building strong relationships can provide access to mentorship and guidance, job opportunities, collaborations, and partnerships that can help individuals succeed in their careers. By being proactive, building trust, being strategic, and staying connected with others in your network, you can cultivate relationships that can lead to valuable opportunities for growth and advancement in your career.

Chapter 18: Social Media and Online Etiquette

- TEACHING RESPONSIBLE social media behavior and online etiquette

In today's digital age, social media has become an integral part of our daily lives. With the click of a button, we can instantly connect with friends and family, share our thoughts and opinions, and access a wealth of information. However, while social media has its benefits, it also comes with its own set of challenges, including the need for responsible behavior and online etiquette.

Teaching responsible social media behavior and online etiquette is crucial in today's society, where the lines between online and offline worlds are becoming increasingly blurred. The way we conduct ourselves online can have real-world consequences, from affecting our relationships with others to impacting our professional and personal reputations. As such, it is important to instill in individuals the skills and knowledge needed to navigate the digital landscape thoughtfully and ethically.

One of the key aspects of teaching responsible social media behavior is promoting digital literacy among individuals of all ages. Digital literacy refers to the ability to understand, evaluate, and use digital technologies effectively and responsibly. By equipping individuals with the necessary skills to critically evaluate online information, identify potential risks, and protect their personal information, we can empower them to make informed decisions about their online behavior.

Another important aspect of teaching responsible social media behavior is fostering empathy and respect in online interactions. In the anonymity of the online world, it can be easy to forget that there are real people behind the screens. Teaching individuals to treat others with kindness and respect online can go a long way in fostering a positive and supportive online community. By encouraging individuals to think before they post, consider the impact of their words and actions on others, and practice empathy in their online interactions, we can help create a more inclusive and respectful online environment.

Furthermore, teaching responsible social media behavior also involves educating individuals about the importance of maintaining a positive digital footprint. A digital footprint refers to the trail of data and information that individuals leave behind when they use the internet. This can include everything from social media posts and comments to photos and videos. By helping individuals understand the implications of their online activities and the potential long-term consequences of their digital footprint, we can empower them to take control of their online presence and make informed choices about what they share online.

In addition to promoting responsible social media behavior, it is also important to teach individuals about online etiquette. Online etiquette, also known as netiquette, refers to the code of conduct that governs how individuals should behave online. This includes guidelines on how to interact with others respectfully, how to handle disagreements and conflicts in a constructive manner, and how to protect one's privacy and security online. By educating individuals about online etiquette, we can help them navigate the complexities of the digital world with grace and courtesy. By promoting digital literacy, fostering empathy and respect, educating individuals about their digital footprint, and teaching online etiquette, we can empower individuals to navigate the online world thoughtfully, ethically, and responsibly. Ultimately, by instilling in individuals the skills and knowledge needed to engage with social media and the digital landscape in a responsible manner, we can help create a more inclusive, respectful, and positive online community for all.

- Discussing the impact of social media on relationships

Social media has become a ubiquitous part of modern life, with billions of people around the world using platforms such as Facebook, Twitter, Instagram, and Snapchat to connect with others and share aspects of their lives. While social media has revolutionized the way we communicate and interact with one another, it also has a profound impact on relationships, both positive and negative.

One of the most significant ways in which social media affects relationships is by enabling people to stay in touch with friends and family members who may be far away. Platforms like Facebook make it easy to share updates, photos, and messages with loved ones, regardless of where they are in the world. This can help to strengthen relationships by allowing people to maintain regular contact and stay connected, even when they are physically apart.

However, social media can also have a negative impact on relationships, particularly romantic ones. Studies have shown that excessive use of social media can lead to feelings of jealousy, insecurity, and distrust in relationships. This is often due to the fact that social media allows people to easily connect with others, including ex-partners, and to see what their partners are doing online. This can lead to comparisons and feelings of inadequacy, as individuals may feel pressured to live up to the idealized versions of themselves that they see on social media.

Moreover, social media can also impact relationships by affecting the way that people communicate with one another. In a world where much of our interaction takes place online, it can be easy to misinterpret messages or to communicate in a way that is less personal and meaningful than face-to-face communication. This can lead to misunderstandings, conflict, and a breakdown in communication, which are all detrimental to healthy relationships.

Despite these potential negative impacts, social media can also have positive effects on relationships. For example, platforms like Instagram and Pinterest can be a source of inspiration for couples looking to plan a dream vacation or decorate their home. Social media can also provide a way for couples to share happy memories and experiences with their friends and followers, strengthening their bond and creating a sense of belonging and community. While social media can have negative effects on relationships, such as jealousy and miscommunication, it can also strengthen bonds and create opportunities for connection and growth. By understanding the ways in which social media affects relationships, individuals can work to mitigate the negative impacts and harness the positive aspects of social media to enhance their relationships and build strong, healthy connections.

Chapter 19: Diversity and Inclusion

- EMBRACING DIVERSITY and promoting inclusion in social settings

Diversity and inclusion are essential aspects of creating a welcoming and supportive social environment. Embracing diversity means recognizing and valuing the differences among individuals, whether it be in terms of race, ethnicity, gender, sexual orientation, abilities, or beliefs. It involves celebrating the unique qualities and perspectives that each person brings to the table. In contrast, promoting inclusion means actively working to ensure that everyone feels welcome and accepted in social settings. This can involve creating a safe space where individuals feel empowered to express themselves and be their authentic selves without fear of judgment or discrimination.

One of the key benefits of embracing diversity and promoting inclusion in social settings is the enrichment of experiences and perspectives. When individuals from different backgrounds come together, they bring with them a wealth of knowledge, skills, and ideas that can help to create a more dynamic and creative environment. By fostering a culture that values and celebrates diversity, social settings can become more vibrant and engaging, leading to greater innovation and collaboration. Additionally, by promoting inclusion, social settings can become more welcoming and accessible to all individuals, regardless of their background or identity.

It is important to note that embracing diversity and promoting inclusion is not just about achieving a quota or meeting a diversity target. Rather, it is about creating a culture that values and respects the unique qualities and perspectives of each individual. This requires a commitment to actively listen to and learn from others, seek out diverse perspectives, and challenge assumptions and biases. It also involves creating opportunities for individuals to share their stories and experiences, fostering empathy and understanding among members of the social setting.

In order to effectively embrace diversity and promote inclusion in social settings, it is important to establish clear guidelines and norms that reflect these values. This can involve creating a code of conduct that outlines expectations for behavior and interactions, as well as providing training and resources to help individuals understand and navigate issues related to diversity and inclusion. It is also important to foster a culture of openness and transparency, where individuals feel comfortable speaking up about any instances of discrimination or exclusion.

Another crucial aspect of promoting diversity and inclusion in social settings is fostering allyship and solidarity among members. This means actively supporting and advocating for marginalized or underrepresented individuals, and working together to address systemic issues of discrimination and inequality. By building a strong network of allies, social settings can create a more inclusive and supportive environment for all individuals. By fostering a culture that celebrates diversity, social settings can become more dynamic and vibrant, leading to greater innovation and collaboration. Additionally, by promoting inclusion, social settings can become more welcoming and accessible to all individuals, regardless of their background or identity. By establishing clear guidelines and norms, fostering allyship and solidarity, and actively listening to and learning from others, social settings can work towards creating a more inclusive and equitable society for all.

- Respecting different backgrounds and perspectives

Respecting different backgrounds and perspectives is essential in fostering a diverse and inclusive environment in any setting. It is important to recognize and value the unique experiences, beliefs, and values that individuals from different backgrounds bring to the table. By doing so, we can create a space where people feel accepted, respected, and understood. This is not only beneficial for individuals but also for the overall success and growth of organizations, communities, and society as a whole.

One of the key reasons why it is important to respect different backgrounds and perspectives is because it promotes empathy and understanding. When we take the time to listen to and learn from others who have different backgrounds and perspectives, we are able to gain a deeper understanding of their experiences and the challenges they may face. This, in turn, allows us to develop empathy and compassion for others, which can help build stronger relationships and foster a sense of unity and connection among individuals.

Additionally, respecting different backgrounds and perspectives helps to challenge our own biases and assumptions. We all have preconceived notions and beliefs about others based on their background or perspective. By engaging with individuals from diverse backgrounds, we can expose ourselves to new ideas, beliefs, and ways of thinking that may challenge our own perspectives. This can be uncomfortable at times, but it is necessary for personal growth and development. By being open to different perspectives, we can expand our own worldview and become more tolerant and accepting of others.

Furthermore, respecting different backgrounds and perspectives is important for creating a positive and inclusive work or social environment. When individuals feel respected and valued for who they are, they are more likely to be engaged, motivated, and productive. This leads to better collaboration, creativity, and overall satisfaction among team members. Inclusion and diversity are key drivers of innovation and success in today's fast-paced and interconnected world. By promoting a culture of respect and understanding, organizations can attract and retain top talent from all backgrounds, and foster a sense of belonging that encourages people to bring their whole selves to work.

In order to respect different backgrounds and perspectives effectively, it is important to actively listen to others and seek to understand their point of view. This requires approaching conversations with an open mind, asking questions, and actively engaging in dialogue with others. It is also important to be mindful of our own biases and assumptions and to challenge them when necessary. By being self-aware and open to learning from others, we can create a more inclusive and accepting environment for all individuals. By valuing the unique experiences and beliefs that individuals from diverse backgrounds bring to the table, we can create a more harmonious and accepting world for all. It is up to each of us to take the time to listen, learn, and engage with others who may have different perspectives. By doing so, we can build stronger relationships, foster innovation, and create a more equitable and diverse society. Let us all commit to respecting and celebrating the rich tapestry of backgrounds and perspectives that make us all unique and valuable members of the global community.

Chapter 20: Conclusion

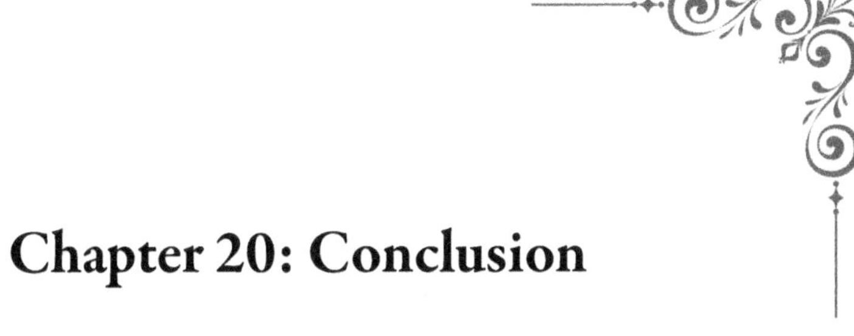

- REFLECTING ON THE progress made in 30 days

Over the past 30 days, there has been significant progress made in various aspects of both personal and professional life. Reflecting upon the accomplishments achieved within this time frame allows for a deeper understanding of growth, challenges overcome, and areas for further improvement. This period of time has provided an opportunity for self-reflection and evaluation of goals set, strategies employed, and outcomes achieved. Through a critical analysis of the progress made, one can gain valuable insights into what has worked well and what can be improved upon in the future.

In terms of personal development, the past 30 days have seen notable progress in areas such as time management, self-care, and goal setting. By prioritizing tasks, creating a daily schedule, and setting clear objectives, there has been a noticeable increase in productivity and efficiency. Engaging in activities that promote self-care, such as exercise, meditation, and healthy eating habits, has also contributed to a sense of well-being and balance. Furthermore, by setting realistic and achievable goals, there has been a clear direction and focus on the desired outcomes, leading to a greater sense of accomplishment and satisfaction.

Professionally, the past month has been a period of growth and advancement in various areas of work and career development. By taking on new challenges, learning new skills, and networking with colleagues and industry professionals, there has been a noticeable improvement in performance and job satisfaction. Setting career goals, mapping out a plan for advancement, and seeking feedback from supervisors and mentors have all contributed to a deeper understanding of career aspirations and the steps needed to achieve them. Additionally, by seeking out opportunities for professional growth and development, such as attending workshops, seminars, and conferences, there has been a steady progression towards achieving long-term career goals.

Reflecting on the progress made in the past 30 days also allows for an evaluation of the challenges faced and how they were overcome. By identifying obstacles, setbacks, and areas of improvement, one can gain valuable insights into areas that require additional attention and focus. By developing strategies to address challenges, seeking support from colleagues and mentors, and remaining resilient in the face of adversity, progress can continue to be made towards achieving personal and professional goals. By reflecting on past experiences, one can also identify patterns of behavior, thought, and action that may be hindering progress and make adjustments as needed to move forward in a positive direction.

Looking ahead, it is important to continue to build upon the progress made in the past 30 days and strive for continued growth and development. By setting new goals, identifying areas for improvement, and seeking out opportunities to learn and grow, one can continue to advance both personally and professionally. By reflecting on past successes and challenges, one can gain valuable insights into areas of strength and areas for improvement, ultimately leading to a more fulfilling and successful life. Through self-reflection, evaluation, and goal setting, one can continue to progress towards achieving long-term goals and aspirations.

- Setting goals for continued growth and improvement in social skills

Setting goals for continued growth and improvement in social skills is an important aspect of personal development. Social skills are essential for success in both personal and professional settings, as they enable individuals to effectively communicate, collaborate, and build relationships with others. By setting specific, achievable goals for improving social skills, individuals can enhance their abilities to navigate social situations with confidence and ease.

One key aspect of setting goals for social skills growth is to first assess one's current strengths and weaknesses in this area. This can be done by reflecting on past social interactions and seeking feedback from trusted friends or colleagues. By identifying areas of improvement, individuals can then set specific, measurable goals that target these areas. For example, if someone struggles with initiating conversations with new people, a goal could be to practice starting conversations with strangers at least once a week.

Another important factor to consider when setting goals for social skills improvement is to make them realistic and achievable. It is important to set goals that are challenging enough to push oneself out of their comfort zone, but not so difficult that they become overwhelming or demotivating. By breaking down larger goals into smaller, more manageable steps, individuals can track their progress and stay motivated to continue working towards their ultimate goal of improved social skills.

In addition to setting specific goals for improvement, it is also important to develop a plan for how to achieve these goals. This may involve setting aside dedicated time each week to practice new social skills, seeking out opportunities to practice in real-life social situations, and seeking feedback from others on their progress. By incorporating these actions into a structured plan, individuals can increase their chances of success and make tangible progress towards their social skills goals.

Furthermore, accountability is an important factor in achieving social skills goals. By sharing their goals with a trusted friend, family member, or mentor, individuals can receive support, encouragement, and feedback to help them stay on track and remain motivated. Peer accountability can also provide a sense of external accountability, as individuals may feel more compelled to take action knowing that others are aware of their goals and progress.

Lastly, it is important to celebrate successes and milestones along the way. Recognizing and rewarding progress towards social skills goals can help individuals stay motivated and encouraged to continue working towards further improvement. By acknowledging the hard work and effort that goes into developing social skills, individuals can build confidence in their abilities and continue to strive for growth and excellence in this area. By assessing current strengths and weaknesses, setting realistic and achievable goals, developing a plan for achievement, seeking accountability and support, and celebrating successes along the way, individuals can enhance their social skills and build stronger relationships with others. Ultimately, by committing to ongoing growth and improvement in social skills, individuals can increase their confidence, effectiveness, and success in both personal and professional settings.